SCHOLARLY WRITING
FOR LAW STUDENTS

SEMINAR PAPERS,
LAW REVIEW NOTES, AND
LAW REVIEW COMPETITION PAPERS

Elizabeth Fajans, Ph.D.
Associate Professor
 of Legal Writing
Writing Specialist
Brooklyn Law School

Mary R. Falk
Associate Professor
 of Legal Writing
Brooklyn Law School

WEST GROUP

Bancroft-Whitney • Banks-Baldwin • Clark Boardman Callaghan
Lawyers Cooperative Publishing • WESTLAW® • West Publishing

ST. PAUL, MINN., 1995

 TEXT IS PRINTED ON 10% POST CONSUMER RECYCLED PAPER

This book is dedicated to our mothers, Ruth Herbert and Mimi Rockmore, and to our husbands, Omar Lerman and Bob Zimmerman.

It goes without saying.

ACKNOWLEDGMENTS

Brooklyn Law School's Summer Stipend Program supported the development of this book; we are grateful to Dean Joan G. Wexler and former Dean (now Judge) David G. Trager for their generosity and encouragement. We are indebted to many others as well for their support and good ideas. In particular, thanks are due to Professors Margaret A. Berger, Eve Cary, Anne Enquist, Maryellen Fullerton, Jessie Grearson, Bailey Kuklin, Ann C. McGinley, Leo Raskind, Mary Barnard Ray, Jeffrey Stempel, Carrie W. Teitcher, Marilyn R. Walter, and Kristin Woolever; Linda Holmes of the Brooklyn Law School library; our research assistant, G. Hanna Antonsson; and former law students Rhonda Panken, Anthony Ranieri, Angela Thompson, Adam Waldman, and Paul Zimmerman. And Rose Patti, who saw the manuscript and camera copy through so many decisions and revisions, was a perfect angel.

TABLE OF CONTENTS

CHAPTER ONE

SCHOLARLY WRITING
IN LAW SCHOOL

> *"I believe scholarship to be an antidote to the cynical carelessness about truth that advocacy encourages. To be sure, any scholarly achievement is partial, one-sided, transient, and inevitably influenced in its inception and execution by the scholar's habits, preferences, values, and so on.... In my judgment, however, it is a more important fact that every scholarly endeavor, no matter what its subject, aims to state something true...."*
>
> *- Anthony T. Kronman*

A. THE SCHOLARLY ENTERPRISE

In the course of your law school career, you should become a confident practitioner of two very different kinds of legal writing, "instrumental" and "critical" writing.[1] Instrumental writing is the crucial stuff of everyday legal practice: simple office and trial memoranda, routine pleadings, wills, and contracts. In its purest form, it is the memorialization on paper of relatively uncomplicated ideas, often with the help of standard forms and boilerplate language. In contrast, critical writing is innovative and introspective, and the writing process generates as well as records the writer's ideas. Much, though certainly not all, critical writing in the law is scholarly writing—the sharing within the legal community of new ideas about the law.

The most usual vehicle for legal scholarship is the law review article written by a law professor, and the several hundred journals or reviews published by some 150 law schools constitute the major forum for such writing. With the exception of some specialist journals edited by practitioners or faculty, law journals are edited by law students. Not only do these journal members select and edit outside articles, but nearly half the content of an average journal is made up of articles written and edited by them.

Although the selection of law review members was once based exclusively on grades, the great majority of law journals now use a writing competition in the selection process. These competitions typically ask the candidate to write a short scholarly paper based on a "closed universe" of supplied readings.

Thus, as a law student, your first encounter with scholarly writing is likely to be the law review competition. If you are invited to join your journal, you will be further immersed in the writing and editing of scholarly articles. But whether you join law review or not, you will almost certainly be asked to write a seminar or term paper—almost all law schools now require such a paper in the second or third year, thus requiring you to demonstrate competence in critical writing.

Whether you are writing a competition paper, seminar paper, or law review article, this book can help you make the necessary transition from instrumental to critical writing. It proposes specific strategies and techniques for each stage of the writing process, from inspiration to final proofreading. We hope it will help you to minimize anxiety and wheelspinning, to produce work you can be proud of, and (even!) to enjoy the process.

Our first concern is to assure you that the enterprise of scholarly writing is neither boring nor irrelevant. Legal scholarship is increasingly pluralistic and lively, opening up to new voices, new concerns, new disciplines. The past twenty years have seen the emergence of many new directions—among them, Law and Economics, Critical Legal Studies, Legal Storytelling, Feminist Jurisprudence, Law and Literature, Law as Practical Reason, and Law as Interpretation. Although student law review articles and seminar papers have traditionally tended to be less ambitious and theoretical than the contributions of law professors, this seems to be changing, too. The importance of the opening up of legal education to new perspectives was underscored in a statement by the Executive Director of the Association of American Law Schools:

> The education of lawyers must not merely involve the acquisition of knowledge and skills; it must include the cultivation of creative thinking and imagination, an appreciation of the commonality of the human condition, and development of a sense of judgment and responsibility. Hence, lawyering includes the ability to understand and critique existing and emerging visions of the profession in relation to interdisciplinary and multicultural perspectives, the implications of technology, and the consequences of economic globalization.[2]

Moreover, as the preceding quotation suggests, legal scholarship has a real bearing on the future of the profession. Like other professionals, lawyers cannot in good conscience concern themselves only with what is, or even with what works: in order to be creative and responsible members of the community, lawyers also need to think about what might, could, should, and should not be. Legal scholarship allows that free play of intellect and imagination out of which the future of a discipline emerges. Many modern tort and contract doctrines were first articulated in law review articles. Perhaps the most famous example of a scholarship-driven doctrine is the law of privacy, first formulated by Samuel D. Warren and Louis O. Brandeis in their 1890 Harvard Law Review article, *The Right to Privacy*.[3]

Appellate judges routinely cite law review articles (including student notes) as persuasive authority, and look to them not just for information, but for new directions. Chief Judge Judith S. Kaye of the New York Court of Appeals has written:

> I like starting an opinion with good briefs and articles.... I look to law review articles for...the newest thinking on the subject, for a sense of the direction of the law and how the case before us fits within it, for a more global yet more profound perspective on the law and its social context than any individual case presents.[4]

Whether judges look to law reviews for new ideas or for support for their conclusions, their reliance is obvious from any perusal of the recent decisions of any appellate court. What is less obvious, but essential to your understanding of critical writing in the law, is that virtually all legal scholarship is implicitly directed to the decision-makers in our society — legislative and executive as well as judicial. In other words, it is characteristically normative (informed by a social goal) and prescriptive (recommending or disapproving a means to that goal).[5] The goals may be as disparate as economic efficiency and equal distribution of wealth, and the suggested courses of action equally varied, but browsing through the introductions to any random selection of law review articles will reveal legal scholarship's normative/prescriptive core. It is thus a fundamentally rhetorical discourse, seeking to persuade its audience of the rightness of its conclusions.

In this, the law is different from most of the other disciplines you have encountered in undergraduate or graduate school. Literary criticism is largely an interpretive discipline, while the social and natural sciences are not characteristically normative and prescriptive; they do not overtly avow some social goal, and although they frequently deal with theoretical entities, they are often simply descriptive. While description (of the facts and reasoning of a case, e.g.) and interpretation (of a constitutional provision, e.g.) play a part in legal scholarship, they are almost always subordinated to the enterprise of pointing the way to a good goal. Thus, whether you are writing a seminar paper, competition paper, or law review article, a purely descriptive or interpretive approach will rarely be successful.

Finally, critical writing is not only relevant to the present and future course of the law, but it is also relevant to the development of your other legal writing skills. Few documents are so routine that a purely "instrumental" approach is sufficient. You will find that the techniques and strategies of critical thinking, reading, and writing that this book describes—for finding inspiration, drafting, revising, editing, and polishing—are as useful for a complex estate plan, office memorandum, or appellate brief as they are essential to your paper. In fact, a recent study shows that former members value the law review experience at least as much for its enhancement of their writing skills as for its enhancement of their resumes.[6]

B. SEMINAR PAPERS, STUDENT LAW REVIEW ARTICLES, AND LAW REVIEW COMPETITION PAPERS

This book is designed to help you with scholarly/critical legal writing in all of the three formats you will encounter in law school:

law review competition, student law review article, and seminar or term paper. However, for the most part, the three are not treated separately here, because the processes of inspiration, drafting, revising, and polishing are the same for all.

Moreover, the same qualities that make a winning competition paper also characterize an "A" paper and a publishable article. Successful scholarly writing is first of all *original*, in that it says something about the law, no matter how modest, that has not been said before. Second, a good scholarly piece is *comprehensive*—it provides sufficient background material to enable any law-school-educated person to understand it and evaluate the writer's thesis. In this sense, legal scholarship always takes the reader from the known (background) to the unknown (the writer's analysis). Further, any strictly factual or descriptive material must be meticulously *correct*, and the writer's analysis must be *logical*: well and sufficiently reasoned and divided into mutually exclusive, yet related, sections. Finally, a good scholarly paper is *clear* and *readable*, written in a somewhat formal style that avoids both the pompous and the colloquial.

The only real differences among the three formats are in manuscript preparation (e.g., footnotes vs. endnotes) and, more importantly, in scale. Law review notes range in length from 10 to 50 printed pages—approximately 30 to 150 manuscript pages. Seminar papers are typically 20 to 40 manuscript pages long, and competition papers shorter still. Whatever its length or immediate purpose, however, almost all student scholarly writing follows one of two patterns: the analysis of one judicial opinion or the analysis of a development or controversy in the law. The next two sections of this chapter describe these two basic patterns.

Preliminarily, though, a note on terms seems in order here. Some law reviews call a student article analyzing one case a "casenote," while others call it a "case comment," or just a "comment" or "note." Further, some reviews call the analysis of a development or controversy a "comment," and others call it a "note." Faced with this confusing terminology, we decided to call one-case analyses "casenotes" and development/controversy analyses "comments." We refer to casenotes and comments collectively as "articles." We also use "paper" to refer to all three formats covered by this book.

1. *The Comment: Examining One Aspect of the Law*

Scholarly comment on the law covers a wide spectrum: depending on your interests and skills, one place will be right for your contribution. Professor Richard Delgado has identified ten sub-categories of the comment.

> First, there is the "case cruncher"—the "typical" article. This type of article analyzes case law in an area that is confused, in conflict, or in transition. Doctrine is antiquated or incoherent and needs to be reshaped. Often the author resolves the conflict or problem by reference to policy, offering a solution that best advances goals of equity, efficiency, and so forth.

> [2] Next, there is the law reform article. Pieces in this vein argue that a legal rule or institution is not just incoherent, but bad—has evil consequences, is inequitable or unfair. The writer shows how to change the rule to avoid these problems.

> [3] There is also the legislative note, in which the author analyzes proposed or recently enacted legislation, often section by section, offering comments, criticisms, and sometimes suggestions for improvement.

> [4] Another type of article is the interdisciplinary article. The author of an interdisciplinary article shows how insights from another field, such as psychology, economics, or sociology, can enable the law to deal better with some recurring problem....

> [5] There is the theory-fitting article. The author examines developments in an area of law and finds in them the seeds of a new legal theory or tort....

> [6] Discussions of the legal profession, legal language, legal argument, or legal education form yet another category of law review writing....

> [7] There are the bookish, learned dialogues that continue a preexisting debate. These pieces take the

following form: "In an influential article in the W Law Review, Professor X argued Z. Critics, including Professor Y, attacked her view, arguing A, B, and C. This Article offers D, a new approach to the problem of Z (a new criticism, a new way of defending X's position in the face of her critics, a way of accommodating X and her critics, or something of the sort)."

[8]   Another category consists of pieces on legal history. The origins and development of a legal rule or institution may shed light on its current operation or shortcomings. [9]   Similarly, comparative law articles are often valuable and engrossing for many of the same reasons: it will sometimes happen that other legal systems treat a problem more effectively or more humanely than does ours.[7]

Finally, there is the empirical research article, which Professor Delgado deems "in some ways, the most useful of all, if one can manage the logistical problems it presents, because it enables the writer to expand knowledge beyond the armchair confines limiting most legal writing."[8]

The majority of legal scholarship and almost all student scholarly work fits into Professor Delgado's first three categories. These are the traditional modes of scholarship, and work in them is the most appreciated by judges and practicing attorneys. Although as a beginning scholarly writer you will most probably write a "case cruncher," law reform, or legislative comment, you should not rule out the other genres, especially if you have relevant pre-law-school training. In particular, if you have been trained in gathering and analyzing data, an empirical study might be appropriate; Professor Delgado is one of a growing number of scholars who are eager to see legal scholarship venture beyond its traditional "armchair confines." Similarly, if you have a background in history, literature, psychology, philosophy, or political science, an inter-disciplinary study might be right for you, especially if you have the added freedom that seminar papers provide.

Although the ranges of appropriate approach and subject matter are very broad, the scholarly comment itself is increasingly narrow in its focus. So much has been written, so many articles appear each month, that comments on general trends or overviews of entire areas of the law are usually redundant—unless, of course, you are the very first person to see the trend or to propose a new perspective. Thus, the most successful comments tend to be specific, rather than general.

Despite the many and varied approaches to the scholarly comment, its format is surprisingly unitary. The same simple organization underlies articles and papers in every one of Professor Delgado's ten categories. It is a basic four-part structure consisting of an introduction, a background section, an analysis section, and a conclusion. The obligatory introduction of one to several pages describes the subject matter of the comment and plainly states the author's thesis. The introduction also provides an explicit roadmap to the rest of the comment: "Part I sets out X. Part II analyzes X and concludes Y." After the introduction, a second section of the comment provides whatever background a law-school-educated person will need to understand the third, most important, section: the writer's original analysis of the subject matter. A short conclusion, often less than a page in length, summarizes the writer's views; the conclusion also may suggest related issues or ramifications, inviting the reader to further reflection.

Of course, background and analysis may each require more than one section. Background may have both a factual and a methodological component, for example, or the analysis may consist of both a critique of existing approaches and a proposed solution. What is essential to a successful scholarly comment, however, is that the proportions of background and analysis be appropriate to the subject matter. The background section should be specific and comprehensive and not assume any but the most general knowledge of the law, on the one hand, but on the other hand, it should not drive the reader away by unnecessary length and irrelevant detail. The analysis section should be the focal point of the comment; it should be original and closely reasoned, building to a convincing conclusion—not trailing off as the exhausted writer sees the deadline (or the dawn) approaching.

In addition to their basic four-part structure, all scholarly comments on the law share another defining characteristic: the extensive use of footnotes, a distinctive and controversial feature of legal scholarship. Footnotes serve three separate functions in scholarly legal writing, which may help to explain why most writers use so many. First, they document the text, providing both authority and bibliography. Second, footnotes serve to attribute borrowed texts or ideas to their sources, avoiding plagiarism. Third, "textual" footnotes permit the writer to express ideas that do not quite fit the straight and narrow path of traditional legal reasoning. Many footnotes serve the first and second function at once; some serve all three.

Textual footnotes are used for creative digressions, for displays of erudition, and sometimes for personal, even humorous, asides to the reader. Some readers and writers are partial to such footnotes, while others denounce them indignantly as pretentious and distracting. The choice of whether to use textual footnotes copiously or sparingly seems less a matter of principle, however, than simply a matter of personal style.

Readers who are impatient with extensive footnoting, most often practitioners and judges, also tend to find that the length, dense reasoning, and detailed documentation of scholarly comments make them demanding and time-consuming reading. Thus, good ideas too sturdily packaged may not easily find an audience outside of academia. One response by law journals to this problem has been the creation of a new format, the "essay" or "commentary." This is a short, informal, sparingly documented article expressing the author's views, usually on a current controversy. This useful format tends to be the province of well-known scholars, however, and is not (at least not yet) an option for most student scholarly writers. However, even within the more rigorous technical and intellectual constraints of the traditional scholarly comment, it is possible to write a lively and original paper that holds the reader's attention.

2. *The Casenote: Analyzing One Opinion*

Unlike the scholarly comment, the one-case analysis or "casenote" is most often written by law students. It was originally a vehicle for informing law review readers that a significant case had been decided. Traditional casenotes were brief and did little other than describe the case and speculate as to its likely practical impact. Today, however, online and looseleaf services perform these functions more quickly and efficiently than a law review can, and the casenote has become vastly more substantial and sophisticated. Its function now is to provide thoughtful and original evaluation of the decision.

Whether written for a law review competition, as a term paper, or for publication, a successful casenote always looks beyond a court's articulated reasons for its decision and beyond the dissent's articulated reasons for disagreement. It is, therefore, never sufficient to argue that the majority is correct for the very reasons the majority advances, nor is it sufficient to argue that the majority is wrong for the very reasons advanced by the dissent. In sum, your casenote must go beyond paraphrase to analysis. Paraphrase is case-briefing, that important form of "instrumental" legal writing mastered during your first year of law school. Casenote analysis is critical writing—writing about what lies between the lines.

A casenote evaluates both the result and the reasoning of a judicial opinion. The following are examples of the kinds of theses that meticulous analysis can yield.

- The result was correct, but the court proposed no clear standard for guidance in future; XYZ would be a workable standard.

- The result was incorrect; the court creates an exception to a constitutional provision that could swallow the rule.

- The result was correct, but it must be narrowly construed or it will have a chilling effect on remedial measures by the legislature.

- The result was incorrect; further, the court's standard is so complex that the outcome of future cases cannot be predicted; ABC would be a better standard.

- The result was correct, but the court never stated the real reason for its decision, which is X.

- The result was correct, but the court's reasoning obscured the proper inquiry.

- The result was incorrect; the court relied unconsciously on long-repudiated constitutional tenets.

- The result was incorrect; the court failed to consider a significant issue which would have been dispositive.

- The result was correct; however, the decision appears to overrule *sub silentio* an important line of cases.

- The result was incorrect; it will result in an inefficient allocation of resources.

- The result was incorrect; the court misconstrued or misused precedent.

Like the scholarly comment, the casenote has begun to incorporate a broader range of perspectives and interdisciplinary approaches. Successful casenotes have used Feminist, Law and Economics, and Law and Literature analyses, for example. Indeed, one casenote effectively used Legal Storytelling, employing a personal narrative to help explain why a federal court wrongly refused to prohibit state display of the Confederate flag.[9]

Like the comment again, the casenote follows a virtually unvarying four-part pattern: introduction, background, analysis, conclusion. The introduction describes the case and its holding very briefly and plainly states the writer's thesis: "In this note (paper), I argue that...." It also provides a roadmap: "Part I describes X; Part II analyzes Y." As with the comment, background sufficient for a law-school-educated reader follows. In some cases, a careful summary of the facts of the case, its procedural history, and the reasoning of majority, concurrence and dissent is sufficient background. Others may require more, a survey of prior cases for example, or an explanation of the writer's approach or methodology. The heart of a casenote, however, is the analysis, and it too may require more than one section—for example, one section that criticizes the decision and one that outlines a solution. A short conclusion summarizes the analysis and invites the reader to take up the issues raised where the writer ended. Finally, like scholarly comments, casenotes use footnotes for authority, attribution, and supplementary discussion. The sample paper in Appendix C is a casenote.

3. *The Law Review Competition Paper: A Special Case*

The majority of law review competitions require students to write casenotes, and thus you should read carefully the immediately preceding section. There are, however, some important differences between competition papers and other casenotes. Not only are law review competition papers much shorter than articles and seminar papers, but they ordinarily require no original research. Thus, you can skip the first part of Chapter Three, "Gathering Information." (But you should read the second part, "Assimilating Information.") The most important distinction between competition papers and the other scholarly formats, however, is a scary one: competition papers are most often written in a short period of time, sometimes in as little as four days.

Your task will seem less overwhelming and your paper will be better if you focus your analysis on one aspect—even one narrow aspect—of the materials. Do not be too general (unless of course the instructions ask you for an overview), and do not skip around from subject to subject. Do try to find something to say that is both original (not a paraphrase) and logically supportable. Chapter Two is designed to help you find something to say.

A tight schedule requires special writing strategies. First, start writing your draft much earlier than you would start any other assignment, as soon as you can; writing generates ideas. (Of course, you should never begin a draft after just one reading of the materials. Competition entries that are excellent in all other respects will almost certainly be disqualified if the writer misread or misunderstood the materials.) Chapter Four proposes strategies for a getting a draft down on paper.

As you revise your draft, pay particular attention to organization and the use of transitions: this will improve the reader's attitude by making your analysis easy to follow. (See Chapter Four, Part B and Chapter Five, Part D.) If you must choose between polishing your prose and putting your ideas in logical, reader-friendly order, spend the time on organization. Above all, be sure that the proportion of background material to analysis is appropriate: be sure you do not end up with eight careful pages of background and two hasty pages of analysis.

If Bluebook style is required for citations and footnotes (or endnotes), make a serious effort to get it right, but do not become obsessed. Neatness and consistency are impressive qualities even if you do not have your Bluebook style down perfectly. (See Chapter Six for footnoting tips.)

Save at least an hour for a final careful proofreading. Careless mistakes turn your reader off. Put a ruler or sheet of paper under the first line, read it, then move the paper down to the next line. This will force you to read slowly and thus to catch mistakes your eye would otherwise rush by. *Never* count on your computer's spell-checking program to catch all mistakes.

Finally, be certain that you have followed all of the competition instructions: you do not want to be disqualified after all your hard work.

Appendix C is a focused and cogent competition paper—you may want to read it before you begin work on yours.

NOTES

1. *See* Philip C. Kissam, *Thinking (By Writing) About Legal Writing*, 40 VAND. L. REV. 135, 138-41 (1987).

2. Memorandum 93-32 from Carl C. Monk, Executive Vice President and Executive Director, *Association of American Law School*, to Deans of Member Schools 2 (May 18, 1993) (on file with authors).

3. Samuel Warren & Louis Brandeis, *The Right to Privacy*, 4 HARV. L. REV. 193 (1890).

4. Judith S. Kaye, *One Judge's View of Academic Law Review Writing*, 39 J. LEGAL EDUC. 313, 319 (1989).

5. Edward L. Rubin, *The Practice and Discourse of Legal Scholarship*, 86 MICH. L. REV. 1835, 1847, 1851 (1988). The discussion of the normative/prescriptive nature of legal scholarship that follows is inspired by Professor Rubin's article.

6. Max Stier, et al., *Law Review Usage and Suggestions for Improvement: A Survey of Attorneys, Professors, and Judges*, 44 STAN. L. REV. 1467, 1491 (1992).

7. Richard Delgado, *How to Write a Law Review Article*, 20 U.S.F. L. REV. 445, 446-47 (1986).

8. *Id*. at 448.

9. James Forman, Jr., Note, *Driving Dixie Down: Removing the Confederate Flag from Southern State Capitols*, 101 YALE L.J. 505 (1991).

CHAPTER TWO

INSPIRATION: CHOOSING A SUBJECT AND DEVELOPING A THESIS

"When inspiration does not come to me, I go halfway to meet it."

- Sigmund Freud

This chapter is designed to help you with the most difficult and most crucial part of writing your paper: finding something worth saying, a process that entails choosing an interesting, significant, and manageable *subject* and then developing an original *thesis*.

The subject of your paper is, of course, the case or topic it discusses. The thesis is your own analysis of the subject, your personal intellectual "take" or angle on it. But a thesis is not just a point of view or personal opinion—it is an assertion supportable by arguments and evidence. Imagine for example that the subject you have chosen (or which has been assigned) is the rights of voluntarily committed mental patients in your state. Through some preliminary research and the use of some of the brainstorming strategies described in Part B of this chapter, you would then develop your thesis—for example, that the appropriate source of such rights is the common law, not the federal or state constitution.[1]

Choosing and narrowing a subject is the easier process; developing your thesis is trickier and more creative. In neither phase, however, do you need to wait nervously, hoping that inspiration will strike before your first draft is due. This chapter proposes active strategies for *finding* inspiration. As you read this chapter, however, keep in mind that inspiration and research are not neatly separable stages. Some preliminary research is necessary to find a subject, and more focused research is necessary to narrow your subject and find a thesis. Conversely, preliminary brainstorming is necessary to focus your research. Thus, the advice on research offered in Chapter Three complements the techniques described here.

A. CHOOSING A SUBJECT

If you are hoping to write a paper of high quality, you must be satisfied that the subject you choose lends itself to authentic discussion and the development of an original thesis—allowing for a historical, comparative, or interdisciplinary approach, for example, or raising unique policy concerns. Ideally, your choice of subject will be informed equally by your own interests, your audience's needs and concerns, and the requirements of the genre—law review article or seminar paper.

When the choice is yours, begin by paying attention to your own interests and instincts. For instance, writing about an area in which you would like to practice has obvious advantages. But no matter how timely and profound (or simple and do-able) a subject may be, if you do not feel passionately about it—or any way at all about it—then let someone else write about it. Writing about something that simply does not interest you is an invitation to procrastination and mediocrity. Although rocky patches are inevitable, scholarly writing should be overall an enjoyable journey of discovery—not a long dull commute.

This is not to say that all is lost if you are assigned a subject that does not interest you or if none of the available subjects seems thrilling. Even the least promising subject can eventually yield an interesting thesis and an "A" paper, but you will have to work harder and longer at the brainstorming stage.

Of course, your choice of subject (and subsequently, your choice of thesis) must also take your audience into account. The audience for law review articles is diverse: highly specialized academics monitoring the intellectual climate, practitioners looking for litigation strategies, and judges seeking perspective on the cases before them. What this audience shares, though, is the desire to be told with maximum clarity something that is both new and illuminating. Although the audience for your seminar paper may be narrower, it is equally interested in reading about an original view of a significant subject; your professor's purpose in assigning a paper is *not* to see you display only your exam-writing skills of issue identification and rule application.

While as a novice scholarly writer you might not feel confident in taking on the burning issues of our time, neither should you be too timid in your choice of subject. Although only you can assess the needs and interests of your immediate audience, your professor or your law review editors, beware of adopting a too narrow view of what this audience wants to read or publish and be aware of the larger reading community. As the preceding chapter suggests, legal scholarship has become increasingly pluralistic, and you should not feel entirely restricted to traditional subjects. Do not rule out an interdisciplinary study, for example, especially for a seminar paper.

1. *Finding a Subject*

Like so many good things, good subjects often begin in conversation. Talk to your professor, employer, or other mentor. Talk to other students. Find out what issues are "out there," what the current concerns of academics and practitioners are. Your coursebooks are another good source of subjects. The notes and comments that follow the cases are a rich source of open questions.

Looseleaf services like *The United States Law Week*, advance sheets, and legal newspapers are all fine sources, too. In particular, the "Summary and Analysis" section of *Law Week* is a useful and wide-ranging guide to current trends in the law. The online services also have features that identify and summarize current developments in the law: "Hot Topics" on LEXIS and "Highlights" on WESTLAW. A good newspaper or news magazine is another excellent source, because it makes up in context what it might lack in legal analysis. On just one day during the writing of this chapter, *The New York Times* contained some twenty stories that raised legal issues. Among others, there were articles suggesting the following significant subjects, a list that seems broad enough to provide something to interest everyone.

- The rights of unmarried domestic partners in New York City

- The defense of necessity in a medical insurance fraud case

- A state's obligation under its own constitution to end de facto school segregation

- Legislation prohibiting Pennsylvania's universities and colleges from discriminating against the disabled

- The application of the Federal Records Act to White House computer tapes containing electronic mail

- The power of quasi-independent agencies to take positions in court that contravene presidential orders

- Legislation in the Polish Parliament forbidding abortion except in cases of rape, incest, genetic abnormality, or threat to the mother's life

- The legal ramifications of an environment-threatening oil spill

2. *Narrowing Your Subject*

A subject that is significant, timely, and fascinating must also be *manageable* in order to be appropriate. There are two techniques that can help you narrow your subject through systematic exploration. One is to use your imagination like a zoom lens, moving from a "macro" focus on your subject at its greatest level of generality to a "micro" level of greatest detail and specificity.[2]

For example, if you were interested in the newspaper story about the rights of unmarried domestic partners, which concerned an executive order by the Mayor of the City of New York, you might first take a "macro" approach and ask why it is in the first instance that the law privileges some relationships over others. At the level of greatest magnification and specificity, you could focus on the very language of the Mayor's order. In between, you might examine the rights of domestic partners in different jurisdictions or in various legal contexts—insurance, succession to leaseholds, or prison visitation, for example.

A related technique for narrowing your subject is based on the categories of argument, or "topics," of Aristotle's *Rhetoric*, which include some of the most basic ways of thinking about subjects: definition, comparison, causation, and substantiation.[3] If you use these categories to explore systematically an interesting but too broad subject, you may well find a manageable aspect of it. For example, consider again the rights of unmarried domestic partners, analyzed this time by "topic."

Topic	Narrowed Subject
Definition	What constitutes a domestic-partner relationship? How is the family being redefined?
Comparison	Compare domestic-partner rights in New York to those in other jurisdictions, to those flowing from other relationships, etc. Compare executive orders with other possible solutions.
Causation	What is the likely effect of the mayor's order? What prompted it?
Substantiation	Executive orders are a good (bad) approach because....

Once you have tentatively settled on an important and manageable subject that interests you, you will need to do a careful search of legal periodicals to determine what has already been written on your subject. Be sure to do a thorough job, using online full-text searches as well as the several indexes in hard copy and online or CD-ROM form. (See Chapter Three, "Research Strategies.") If a truly daunting amount has already been written on your subject, capitulation might be in order. On the other hand, it is almost always possible to carve out a niche for yourself by developing a novel thesis. Finally, if you are writing a casenote, check to see whether further litigation or legislative or executive action threatens your decision with mootness.

B. DEVELOPING A THESIS

"The impulse to write comes from the discovery of a comment worth making."
                                    - Richard L. Larson

Once your preliminary research has enabled you to narrow an interesting and significant subject to manageable proportions, the next major step—perhaps the hardest step—is to find a thesis, an original and supportable proposition about the subject.

A thesis, like a subject, should be manageable. You do not need to resolve an entire area of law that is in turmoil. Your goal can be more modest. Professor Delgado suggests that you "find one new point, one new insight, one new way of looking at a piece of law, and organize your entire article around that. One insight from another discipline, one application of simple logic to a problem where it has never been made before is all you need."[4]

It is reassuring to realize that papers are often built around a single insight. It is equally reassuring to realize that insights are usually not the fortuitous product of inspiration. Rather, insight begins in simple observation, in noting the obvious. Imagine that you notice that a judge uses the word "concededly" a lot in his opinions. Then you notice that the points that follow the adverb "concededly" are very rarely concessions that the parties made or would be likely to make. Only then, on the basis of these two observations, can you infer—have the insight—that the judge is using language in ways that discourage critical probing into his logic.[5] Observations—not the Muses or Fates—are, most normally, the sources of insight and understanding.

Yet, however modest the origins of your eventual thesis, it is helpful to begin thinking about possible theses as early as possible. Although many people seem to separate the research stage from the thinking and writing stages, this is an artificial, and perhaps even destructive, distinction. If you have been taking notes that summarize your research, but do not include in your notes tentative thesis possibilities, gut reactions, and reflections, your final job of selecting a thesis and synthesizing your research may seem overwhelming. Moreover, a provisional thesis can provide helpful direction to your research, although you must be careful to prevent a tentative thesis from blinding you to contrary evidence that requires you to refine or abandon it.

Because a thesis is so central to the enterprise of scholarly writing, the rest of this chapter describes brainstorming techniques that may help you find one.

1. Reading Critically

> *"Analysis is always an account of what is not visible in the text."*
> *- Joseph M. Williams*

One of the best ways to search for a thesis is to be a critical reader. Critical reading requires you to do more than summarize. It demands more than basic understanding of the author's ideas and arguments. Rather, critical reading requires you to ask questions, to play the devil's advocate. To embark on this kind of critical analysis, you must consider what is not said in a text as well as what is said. This means you must both probe the text itself for hidden meanings and go beyond the text to locate it in the legal, historical, social, and political contexts that may help you to understand it. These approaches are particularly helpful in reading judicial opinions, but they enrich the reading of all sources.

a. Probing the Text

i. Take a Problem-Solving Approach

Karl Llewellyn believed that the best way to analyze a judicial opinion was not just to extract issue-holding-reasoning, but to imagine the case as a problem to be solved—that is, to go back and recreate the litigation in your mind, imagining every possible argument that could have been made by the parties.[6] If you are writing a casenote, Llewellyn's technique can help you find something to say about your case.

Imagine, for example, that the preliminary research inspired by the domestic-partner newspaper article has led you to a case that you believe worthy of a casenote or seminar paper. This decision holds that the life partner of a biological mother is not a "parent" within the meaning of the Domestic Relations Law and therefore has no standing to seek visitation with a child jointly raised, because the decisions of a fit parent traditionally have legal priority over the wishes of third parties.[7] Just imagining arguments that might have been made could put you well on the way toward a thesis. It might be argued, for instance, that the best interests of the child mandate visitation rights, that child and life partner both have constitutional rights to establish family relationships and that these rights are compromised by denial of visitation, or that the biological parent is equitably estopped from forbidding visitation. Any one of these arguments could inform the thesis of an interesting casenote.

ii. Read for Jurisprudence

Reading for jurisprudence—analyzing the way the writer looks at law and justice, legal interpretation, or adjudication—is another way of probing a text. Every age has a roughly definable mainstream jurisprudence; in ours, Formalist,[*] Legal Realist,[†] Legal Process,[‡] and Fundamental Rights[§] movements converge. Yet as the century closes, there are many other influential and competing views of the law—for example, Law and Economics,[**] Critical Legal Studies,[††]

---

[*]   Formalists see law as a set of fixed general principles from which conclusions as to specific cases can be deduced. For a Formalist judge, adjudication is largely a matter of deriving the appropriate rule from precedent and applying it without regard to morality or public policy.

[†]   Legal Realists see law and adjudication in social, political, historical, and economic contexts. Legal Realist judges tend to be willing to consider empirical evidence as well as precedent and often reach conclusions by balancing the equities.

[‡]   Legal Process jurisprudence arose largely from the perception that Legal Realism is not a predictable approach to adjudication. Legal Process judges emphasize rationality, restraint, and fairness -- especially fair notice and opportunity to be heard. In essence, Legal Process seeks to reconcile Formalism and Legal Realism.

[§]   Fundamental Rights theory tends to privilege basic notions of justice and human dignity over concerns for neutrality, judicial restraint, and predictability.

[**]   Law and Economics jurisprudence uses microeconomics to analyze almost every aspect of the law. The analysis, however, varies according to the writer's particular economic theory. Most early Law and Economics scholars were associated with the conservative "Chicago School," which valued efficiency and maximization of social wealth. More recent scholarship is more eclectic.

[††]   Critical Legal Studies (CLS) is a descendant of Legal Realism. CLS scholars argue that law is fundamentally indeterminate, and that its purported neutral principles inevitably favor the privileged and fail the underprivileged -- in short, that law is politics.

and Feminist Jurisprudence.[‡‡] This is a time of engaged and far-ranging debate, an exciting time to be studying and writing about the law.

The germ of a casenote thesis can often be found by analyzing the jurisprudential approach taken by the court in your case and then imagining how taking different approaches would affect the outcome and inform the reasoning. Suppose for example that you are going to write a casenote on *Milligan-Jensen v. Michigan Technological University*,[8] a sex-discrimination case decided by the Sixth Circuit Court of Appeals. The plaintiff in that case, the University's only woman security guard, was consistently assigned the worst work shift, which her supervisor jeeringly called the "lady's job." After unsuccessfully requesting reassignment, the plaintiff filed a complaint with the Equal Employment Opportunity Commission. The University then fired her, and she added a second cause of action, retaliation, to her complaint. During discovery, it was determined that the plaintiff had lied on her initial application, failing to inform the employer of a driving-under-the-influence conviction.

Determining that the plaintiff had been illegally discriminated and retaliated against by her employer, the Sixth Circuit nonetheless granted summary judgment to the University. The court reasoned that the University required a clean record and the plaintiff violated that rule. Therefore, according to the court, she was not a legitimate employee and could not claim damages under a statute enacted to protect employees.

Resolving the issue in these terms, the court took a Formalist approach, dispassionately applying law to fact with no regard to legislative intent, social context, or public policy. A judge practicing conservative Law and Economics would reach the same result as the Sixth Circuit did, but by a very different route, concluding that if the plaintiff prevailed, there would be an unreasonable economic burden placed on employers, who would have to check all statements made on applications.

But a judge following the more liberal Yale School of Law and Economics might find for the plaintiff, reasoning that such an

---

[‡‡] As well as seeking fair treatment of women under the law and fair representation within the profession, Feminist Jurisprudence criticizes traditional legal reasoning, hierarchy, and discourse practices.

outcome would deter sexually hostile work environments and thus prevent productivity losses attributable to such conditions. A Legal Realist would also be likely to find for the plaintiff, balancing the equities, looking to the intent behind the statute, and calling on "common sense." By these measures, the Legal Realist would conclude that the statute was meant to help mistreated employees like the plaintiff and that her employer's actions were more blameworthy than her omission. Judges practicing Feminist or Critical Legal Studies jurisprudence would without doubt find for the plaintiff, privileging progressive legislation over punitive regulations imposed on the powerless plaintiff. Both would undoubtedly also consider that her victory was small compensation for a life lived in a fundamentally inequitable society. Judges following still other jurisprudential currents would advance still other bases for one or the other outcome.

The point of this simplified sketch of contemporary jurisprudence is that in analyzing a judicial opinion, there is far more to think about than whether a court "correctly" applied or construed the law. Examining the court's understanding of the nature of law, interpretation, and adjudication can take your analysis deeper and help you find something worth saying.

iii. Read for Inconsistency and Omission

Sometimes there are incompatibilities between what a text promises and what it delivers. The writer may spend more time on what she wants to reject or eliminate than on what she claims to resolve, or she may neglect an important aspect of the problem. For instance, a writer may purport to show that warrantless administrative searches of business premises do not violate the fourth amendment, but all that writer actually shows is that the government has a substantial interest in such searches. An inconsistency like this might yield a thesis.

Another kind of inconsistency results when a court's or an author's assertions are not legitimately supported by the authorities cited. For example, in holding that religious beliefs did not excuse the respondents from compliance with an otherwise valid and generally applicable law, the Supreme Court in *Employment Division v. Smith*[9] cited as binding precedent an overruled decision, neglecting to indicate that it was overruled. This misuse of authority became the thesis of an article arguing that the Court's real reasons for changing First Amendment free exercise of religion doctrine were buried under a misleading "adherence-to-precedent" rationale.[10]

Indeed, judicial opinions often fail to set out the real reasons for a decision. As former Arkansas Supreme Court Justice Robert A. Leflar writes, overcrowded dockets often prevent judges from thinking through ground-breaking decisions and this prompts them to offer "authority reasons" where substantive reasons would be more appropriate.[11] Substantive reasons go to the ultimate merits of the controversy and fall into one of two primary categories. "Goal reasons" justify a decision on the ground that it will promote desired social ends like public health or fair labor practices. "Rightness reasons" justify a decision on the basis of accepted socio-moral norms and look to such equitable matters as culpability and fair dealing.

Often a thesis will emerge if you can articulate the court's unspoken, but real, reason for a decision. Your paper can focus on the impact these unspoken reasons have on the argument's viability or the decision's usefulness. For example, in *Braschi v. Stahl Associates*,[12] another important case that preliminary research on the "domestic-partner" issue would have found, the New York Court of Appeals held that the term "family" in a noneviction provision of the rent-control laws includes adult life partners unrelated by blood or law whose relationship is characterized by emotional and financial commitment and interdependence. The court offered "goal reasons" to support its redefinition. It said it was bringing rent control law in line with the reality of contemporary family life. In so doing, the court almost invited the legal community to expect this definition to be extended to allied areas of law.

In its opinion, the Court of Appeals, unlike the lower courts, nowhere mentioned that the tenant of record died of AIDS in a city in which thousands of other HIV-positive unmarried life partners also lived in rent-regulated apartments to which only traditional "family" had previously had succession rights. A reader alert to the court's silence might have wondered whether compassion for AIDS victims was in any way behind the court's surprising judicial activism— whether, in other words, "rightness reasons" rather than "goal reasons" were the true basis of the court's decision. And if the redefinition of family *was* motivated largely by sympathy for desperately ill people facing eviction, rather than an interest in making law more responsive to contemporary notions of family, your paper could examine whether the court would be likely to extend that definition to other contexts. A reader who questioned *Braschi* thus could have correctly predicted in a casenote that the court would not extend its remarkable decision in *Braschi* beyond the housing context.

In addition to demanding consistency and candor, you should also ask a text about its silences. Sometimes opposing arguments are not raised or addressed, or there are important gaps in reasoning that confuse or even undermine an argument; if you can reconstruct these arguments, you may have found your thesis. For example, the thesis of the sample law review competition paper in Appendix C was generated by the writer's observation of a gap in the court's reasoning: the court begged the question of whether recitation of the Pledge of Allegiance by school children is more like curriculum than like prayer. Sometimes, too, one party's story overshadows the other's in a judicial opinion. Exploring the story of the party who was silenced can help you to better understand and evaluate the equities.[13]

iv. Read for Rhetoric and Style

Another way of probing the text is to read for rhetoric and style. Literary critics believe that texts have multiple meanings, meanings beyond those an author intended. Thus, you should not just take writers "at their word," but should analyze their style and rhetorical strategies in order to have a greater understanding of what is actually going on in a text. Rather than simply agreeing with a writer's position because it is superficially reasonable, therefore, you should examine the undercurrents—the writer's assumptions about and attitude toward the subject matter and the reader—to decide if agreement is really warranted.

In particular, you can learn a lot about a writer by taking a close look at her tone-of-voice and use of words and figures of speech. For example, in *Board of Education v. Dowell*,[14] the Supreme Court held that an injunction in a school desegregation case may be dissolved upon a sufficient showing that the school board "complied in good faith with the desegregation decree since it was entered...[if] the vestiges of past *de jure* segregation ha[ve] been eliminated to the extent practicable." In its opinion, the majority analogizes the Oklahoma City Board of Education to a poor student "condemned" to the foreign "tutelage" of the District Court "for the indefinite future." Thus, through a simple metaphor likening judicial supervision to harsh schooling, the former wrong-doer takes on the innocence of the victim: the School Board, not the African-American student, labors under "draconian" tutelage, and the reader is pushed to regard the Board, the oppressor in *Brown v. Board of Education*,[15] as the oppressed in *Dowell*. This kind of rhetorical pressure may affect our view of the merits of a debate—especially if we are unaware of it. Being aware of it can also point the way to a thesis.

In addition to incidental figures of speech like the *Dowell* example, the law also abounds in figures of speech that have become institutionalized as doctrine. First Amendment law is dominated by such expressions—"chilling effect," "marketplace of ideas," and "public forum." Cautious courts warn of "slippery slopes" and gaping "floodgates" and require legislation to pass "constitutional muster." Recently, scholars have begun to analyze these judicial figures of speech;[16] perhaps critical examination of expressions that you have come to take for granted can help point you in the direction of a thesis. Take, for example, the "open fields" doctrine in Fourth Amendment law. It holds, in essence, that there is no constitutionally protected expectation of privacy in undeveloped land. What is the effect on the reader of calling all undeveloped land, even wooded ravines and junkyards, "open fields"? Does the doctrine seem as incontrovertible when we look at its language up close? Taking a long hard look at language very often generates ideas, and even whole critiques.

b. Probing the Context

In addition to closely analyzing the text itself, it is often profitable to examine its legal and historical context. For example, although lawyers, law students, and law professors tend to write about appellate decisions rather than trial court decisions, there can be no proper assessment of those higher court decisions without a close look at the lower court proceedings. In order to justify its decision, an appellate court may well describe a case and its decision quite differently from those who have worked on the case at a lower court level, though even a trial court opinion molds and condenses the transcript by transforming the original event into a legal incident for judgment.[17] These acts of transformation often result in simplification and omission. Thus, to assess an appellate decision, it is important to read the lower court decisions, as well as any available transcripts or other reliable accounts of the facts.

Moreover, some decisions are not fully understandable without looking at the historical context in which they arose. In *Minersville School District v. Gobitis*,[18] for example, the Supreme Court held that a pupil, a Jehovah's Witness, was not deprived of due process or religious liberty by a requirement that all students salute the flag in public school. Yet, only three years later, *Gobitis* was

overruled in *West Virginia State Board of Education v. Barnette*.[19]
To understand *Gobitis* and *Barnette*, you must look into their social
and historical context.[20] *Gobitis* was decided in 1940, when Nazi
Germany was at its strongest, and America's response was, in part,
to increase displays of patriotic behavior like flag salutes. In rejecting
the petition of Jehovah's Witnesses in *Gobitis*, the Court
unintentionally but tragically branded that sect as unpatriotic. As a
result, in the early 1940s, Witnesses were discriminated against and
physically brutalized, and the Court soon found itself and its decision
criticized by Congress, the ABA, the press, and the lower federal
courts.[21] Thus, when *Barnette* overruled *Gobitis* just three years
later, the Justices were responding at least in part to political and
social unrest.

Of course, the Court in *Barnette* did not refer to this rampant
disapproval, and a reader of only the decision itself would be unaware
of the widespread distress that *Gobitis* engendered[22] and mystified
by its rapid overruling. Putting the law in context can clarify
ambiguous or anomalous developments and give you something
important to write about.

2. *Keeping a Reading Journal*

> *"The meaning of what [one] reads or writes resides
> not in the page nor in the reader but in the encounter
> between the two."*
>   *- Mina P. Shaughnessy*

When you read, thoughts begin to percolate. At first, this
thinking may be subliminal. But as you get into a text and a subject,
as you read closely and critically, thoughts erupt into consciousness.
When this happens, reading is no longer simply about piecing out the
arguments of the author you are reading; it is also about your
reactions to those arguments, to that text. It is important to preserve
the thoughts generated by both your spontaneous and your critical
readings because a thesis may emerge from them. Therefore, you
may want to keep a reading journal while you are researching your
project.

Journals differ from note-taking in that notes typically tend to
be summaries of what an author says, rather than a record of what the
reader thinks about what the author is saying. Yet a reader who
focuses exclusively on what a text says will never produce a paper
which is more than a readable paraphrase or summary of his or her

research. To write a critical analysis, you must preserve your own thinking about another person's thinking.

A double-entry journal is one useful kind of reading journal. On the left-hand page of a notebook, summarize the substance of the piece. On the opposite page, record your responses and reactions to what is said. The example below is an excerpt from a reading journal kept by the writer of the sample law review competition paper in Appendix C. In it, the writer takes notes on and records her ideas about *Sherman v. Community Consolidated District 21*,[23] where the Seventh Circuit held that recitation of the Pledge of Allegiance by willing public school children does not unconstitutionally coerce children who wish not to pledge.

Notes	Reactions
U.S. Sup. Ct. held gov't. can't compel recitation of Pledge (<u>Barnette</u>, 1943). But 1979 Ill. Stat. says "Pledge of Allegiance shall be recited each school day by pupils in [public] elementary educational institutions...."(439). Ct. says stat. O.K. because "pupils" means "willing pupils." Then it frames the issue here: whether child who objects to reciting pledge can "prevent others from reciting it in his presence?" (<u>Id</u>.) Ct. says no....	Shall = duty? <u>Very</u> young children... does it matter? Statutory interpretation O.K.? Is this how plaintiff framed the issue?

Another technique is to use looseleaf paper to take notes. Then file your ideas and reflections in a separate section of a three-ring binder. File cards are useful only if they are large enough to hold quotes from your sources and your reflections on them. If you use a computer, you could write your responses on the alternate screen. What is essential, even at this early stage, is to distinguish your ideas from your meticulously quoted sources, and thus avoid the risk of inadvertent (but no less inexcusable) appropriation of words or ideas that are not your own. (See Chapter Six, Part B.)

Whatever method you use, the important task is to record your responses to what is said. At a minimum, this requires noting down your questions, initial evaluations, associations, and gut reactions as you do your preliminary reading. Also jot down useful words, phrases, sentences, even whole paragraphs that come to you. Do not censor yourself, and do not discard any of your raw material. These jottings could be the seeds of your thesis, and even find their way into the paper itself. Writing can, even should, begin with your research, with your reading.

You may find it helpful to reread your journal on a regular basis in order to determine whether any dominant themes, questions, or arguments are emerging. If so, note them down. For example, a reading journal that contains many personal associations or gut reactions may indicate that the text makes sense or fails to make sense depending on whether the reader shares the value system of the author. If, on the other hand, the reading journal is full of references to possible logical inconsistencies, or to gaps or ambiguities in the law or in an argument, you could try to write out the missing arguments. If you are able to fill the gaps in the argument or explain away the inconsistencies (as a matter of semantics, perhaps), you have potentially found the "problem" that the paper can explicate. If the gaps cannot be filled or the inconsistencies resolved, then you have grounds for a critique. Or perhaps you have recorded a number of factual questions about your case or topic; the next step might be close examination of, say, the lower court proceedings or relevant secondary source material. This might develop into a sort of "context" approach to the subject.

3. *Experimenting with Freewriting*

> *"The habit of writing thus for my eye only is good practice. It loosens the ligaments .... The main requisite ... is not to play the part of censor, but to write as the mood comes or of anything whatever...."*
> *- Virginia Woolf*

> *"I write to find out what I think."*
> *- John Ashbery*

The best papers have something original to say. Unfortunately, originality is hard to come by. Most of us have to work to achieve it. We have to explore, to experiment, to play with content—often for extended periods of time—before we come up with a workable and creative idea for a paper. Freewriting is a good way to ward off "premature closure"[24] of the brainstorming process.

Freewriting asks you to focus on a topic and to write down, in a stream-of-consciousness mode, whatever comes to mind. In freewriting, you do not worry about how you appear to your reader—you are your only reader. You forget about grammar, style, and spelling. Digressions are fine; they may even lead to something fruitful. Usually, after a page or so, valuable phrases, comparisons, and specific thoughts emerge.

Invisible writing is a variation on freewriting that you might try if you use a computer for your writing. Just turn off your computer screen.[25] Released from the distracting habit of editing and amending the text as it is being written, your creative juices may flow; it is often helpful to separate the process of generating ideas from the process of perfecting text.

You should approach freewriting with the spirit of experiment, and you should experiment with your freewriting. In the early stages of a project, you freewrite to generate ideas, not final drafts. Completion is yet a distant prospect. You will probably find that these early musings are wide-ranging and unfocused. Do not worry about this. Just pick up a pen or sit down at the computer, focus on your topic, and begin to write. If you cannot think of anything to say, write that. Keep repeating it until another thought comes into your mind. Continue this process for fifteen to forty-five minutes.

After this time, stop writing, reread, and think about your work.[26] Write down any important idea that has emerged. Make guesses about what your first musings were trying to add up to. Note contradictions, implications, questions. Write down any new thoughts you have in response to what you wrote. Then write a sentence or two that summarizes the focus of your first freewriting —whether it be an assertion, a mood, a question. Once you have summed up your first exercise, start writing again. Your second freewriting exercise should take off from the summing up sentence of your first exercise. You can repeat this process until you are satisfied that some profitable ideas have emerged.[27]

Once some ideas and themes have emerged, you may want to undertake more focused types of freewriting. If you are writing a casenote, you could try brainstorming one of the theses listed in

Chapter One, Part B(2). Or you could freewrite on specific knotty problems you are confronting. Make lists of every aspect of an issue. Examine these aspects by freewriting from varying points of view. Work up first impressions. Write about the problems you are having writing.

Play with words and punning. Encourage analogies and metaphors: a fresh analogy can turn into a thesis. A student who was freewriting on a decision discussed earlier in this chapter, *Board of Education v. Dowell*, began to muse about how *Dowell* would "wipe out" *Brown v. Board of Education*, the landmark school desegregation decision. "Or more accurately," he punned, "*Dowell*—if not a 'black out'—seems to be a *Brown*-out." Not only did his paper come to focus on this power-failure analogy, *Dowell* as the weakening, the dimming, the *Brown*ing-out, of the earlier decision, but the freewrite was also the source of a clever title.

Freewriting does not usually produce chronological narratives or linear arguments, however. Indeed, sometimes the significance of a freewriting exercise is not immediately apparent. Yet often, according to one writing teacher, this kind of brainstorming leads to conceptual breakthroughs like the following, which may commit you to major rethinking.

- In trying to argue X, you become convinced Y is right. It took working through X to appreciate Y.

- In struggling to evaluate the merits of X and Y, you come up with Z, an even better idea.

- In rereading your freewriting, a digression or subpoint takes on sudden significance. You decide this could be the focus of your paper rather than a peripheral point.

- In the middle of writing, you suddenly see what you have been trying to get at.

- In looking over your work, you see your good idea is not good. Some time later, you realize parts of that idea can be salvaged.[28]

Freewriting can be part of your reading journal. After finishing a text, spend a few minutes freewriting about it. When rereading your journal entries, freewrite about possible connections or disparities between the texts. These raw reactions, these observations, are grist for the mill. For an example of freewriting, see Chapter Four, Part A(1).

4. *Still Fishing? Final Thoughts*

If you have tried all these techniques and you still do not have a thesis, try to figure out why. Perhaps your subject is not really a good fit for you. If so, do not cling to it stubbornly: try again.

Perhaps you feel too much has already been written on the topic. Try listing other authors' theses on the topic and then search for a niche between the previous papers,[29] that is, search for an issue raised but not dwelt upon. One student article on software copyright infringement cases is a good example of "niche" finding. The author realized that copyright law lacked a workable system of definitions of software program parts, although some commentators had noted that a test proposed by Learned Hand in a different context seemed relevant to computer programming. The student author's "niche" was to propose computer program definitions that developed that test to make it useful in software infringement cases.[30] In addition to finding theses in the gaps between articles, as this author did, you might also find issues in the textual footnotes of law review articles.

There is nothing wrong with developing another writer's idea, or putting it in a new context, as long as you give credit to the source of your inspiration. Indeed, some of the most distinguished works of scholarship had just such a beginning. For example, James Boyd White, a well-known law-and-literature scholar, begins an important article by explaining that it was inspired in part by a colleague's lecture.[31]

Finally, if you have a provisional thesis but are just not satisfied that it works (or even if you think it does work), there is one last strategy, perhaps the most agreeable of all: take a rest. When writers take time away from an intellectual problem, even as little as half an hour, a process of "incubation" takes place and they often come back to the problem with a stronger solution. The explanation for this phenomenon seems to be that writers tend to formulate a thesis and then try to fit all subsequently learned information into it. When this does not work, progress seems blocked. But if they take some time off (but not so much that the problem goes stale), they forget or abandon the ineffective parts of their thesis and are able to revise it to fit the new information.[32]   One practical reason for starting your paper early, then, is that instead of panicky wheel-spinning when you are stuck in the mud, you can take a relaxing break by the side of the road while your car gets itself out of the rut.

REFERENCES FOR FURTHER READING

PETER ELBOW, WRITING WITHOUT TEACHERS, Oxford Univ. Press (1973); WRITING WITH POWER: TECHNIQUES FOR MASTERING THE WRITING PROCESS, Oxford Univ. Press (1981).

ROBERT L. FERGUSON, *The Judicial Opinion As Literary Genre*, 2 YALE J.L. & HUMAN. 201 (1990).

CAROLYN HEILBRUN, & JUDITH RESNIK, *Convergences: Law, Literature, & Feminism*, 99 YALE L.J. 1913 (1990).

BAILEY KUKLIN, & JEFFREY W. STEMPEL, FOUNDATIONS OF THE LAW, West (1994).

ROBERT A. LEFLAR, *Honest Judicial Opinions*, 74 NW. U. L. REV. 721 (1979).

GARY MINDA, *Jurisprudence At Century's End*, 43 J. LEGAL EDUC. 27 (1993).

GARY MINDA, POSTMODERN LEGAL MOVEMENTS: THE STATE OF THE LAW AND JURISPRUDENCE AT CENTURY'S END, N.Y.U. Press (1995).

JAMES BOYD WHITE, *Judicial Criticism*, 20 GA. L. REV. 835 (1986).

NOTES

1.   *See* Judith S. Kaye, *Foreword: The Common Law and State Constitutional Law as Full Partners in the Protection of Individual Rights*, 23 RUTGERS L. REV. 727, 746-47 (1992).

2.   *See* Sarah W. Sherman, *Inventing an Elephant: History as Composition*, in ONLY CONNECT: UNITING READING AND WRITING 217-20 (Thomas Newkirk, ed. 1986).

3.   ARISTOTLE, THE RHETORIC, (Lane Cooper trans., 1932); *see also* LINDA FLOWER, PROBLEM SOLVING STRATEGIES FOR WRITING 74-75 (1981).

4.   Richard Delgado, *How to Write a Law Review Article*, 20 U.S.F. L. REV. 445, 448 (1986).

5.   This insight belongs to Richard Weisberg, *How Judges Speak: Some Lessons On Adjudication* In Billy Budd, Sailor, *With An Application To Justice Rehnquist*, 57 N.Y.U. L. REV. 1 (1982).

6.   *See* Karl Llewellyn, *The Current Crisis in Legal Education*, 1 LEGAL EDUC. 211, 213 (1948).

7.   In Re Alison D. v. Virginia M., 572 N.E.2d 27 (N.Y. 1991).

8.   975 F.2d 302 (6th Cir. 1992). This example and the analysis that follows are adapted from BAILEY KUKLIN & JEFFREY W. STEMPEL, FOUNDATIONS OF THE LAW 52-57 (1994).

9.   494 U.S. 872 (1990).

10.   *See* Michael W. McConnell, *Free Exercise Revisionism and the Smith Decision*, 57 U. of CHI. L. REV. 1109 (1990).

11.   Robert A. Leflar, *Honest Judicial Opinions*, 74 NW. U. L. REV. 711, 721 (1979). *See also*, Robert S. Summers, *Two Types of Substantive Reasons: The Core of a Theory of Common-Law Justification*, 63 CORNELL L. REV. 707 (1978).

12.   543 N.E. 2d 49 (N.Y. 1989).

13.   *See* Legal Storytelling, 878 MICH. L. REV. (1989), a symposium volume on the importance of legal storytelling.

14.   498 U.S. 237 (1990)

15.   349 U.S. 294 (1955).

16.   *See, e.g.*, HAIG BOSMAJIAN, METAPHOR AND REASON IN JUDICIAL OPINIONS (1992).

17.   *See* Carolyn Heilbrun & Judith Resnik, *Convergences: Law, Literature, and Feminism*, 99 YALE L.J. 1913 (1990).

18.   310 U.S. 586 (1940).

19.   319 U.S. 624 (1943).

20.   For an interesting analysis of these cases, *see* Robert A. Ferguson, *The Judicial Opinion as Literary Genre*, 2 YALE J.L. & HUMAN. 201 (1990).

21.   Heilbrun & Resnik, *supra* note 17, at 1939.

22. *Id.* at 1940.

23. 980 F.2d 437 (7th Cir. 1992).

24. *See* Lynn Hammond, *Using Focused Freewriting to Promote Critical Thinking*, *in* NOTHING BEGINS WITH N: NEW INVESTIGATIONS OF FREEWRITING 72 (Pat Belanoff *et al*, eds. 1991).

25. *See* Sheridan Blau, *Thinking and the Liberation of Attention: The Uses of Free and Invisible Writing*," in NOTHING BEGINS WITH N, *supra* note 24, at 283.

26. *See* Peter Elbow, WRITING WITHOUT TEACHERS (1973), (seminal work on freewriting).

27. *Id.* at 19-22.

28. ELBOW, *supra* note 26, at 36-37.

29. *See* MARY B. RAY & BARBARA J. COX, BEYOND THE BASICS: A TEXT FOR ADVANCED LEGAL WRITING 408 (1991).

30. John W.L. Ogilvie, Note, *Defining Computer Program Parts Under Learned Hand's Abstractions Test in Software Copyright Infringement Cases*, 91 MICH. L. REV. 526 (1992).

31. James B. White, *Judicial Criticism*, 20 GA. L. REV. 835 (1986).

32. *See* FLOWER, *supra* note 3, at 77-78.

CHAPTER THREE

RESEARCH STRATEGIES

At the heart of the research process there is a seemingly insoluble chicken-and-egg problem: you need a thesis to focus your research, but you cannot focus your thesis without doing research. Yet the problem is only insoluble if we consider inspiration, research, and writing as neatly separable stages of the critical writing process. In fact, the three do not follow in orderly sequence like the chapters of this book. Rather, the process of critical writing is complex, more like an upward spiral than a straight line. The sequence research-reading-reflection-writing may repeat itself again and again before you have finished your paper: not all circular motion is wheel-spinning.

Yet we can say that there is a part of the process that involves *more* brainstorming than researching and writing, and call that the inspiration stage. Similarly, we can identify a stage that is mostly research, and one that is mostly writing. Thus, it is to the "mostly research" stage that this chapter is addressed, just as the preceding chapter is addressed to the "mostly inspiration" stage and the succeeding chapters address the "mostly writing" stages.

The mostly research stage itself has two major components: gathering information and assimilating it, making it your own through close reading and meticulous note-taking. In general, the process starts with the acquisition of a general overview, often achieved by browsing and skimming, then moves to a compilation of relevant materials, and culminates in critical reading and note-taking. However, it is unrealistic to expect that you can gather all your materials and later work your way through the stack of books, photocopies, and printouts. If you confine your reading in the early stages of research to browsing and skimming, you cannot adequately focus your thesis and direct your subsequent research. Even the first stages must include some close reading and critical reflection.

Thus, although the two following sections of this chapter deal separately with gathering and assimilating information, you should bear in mind that the two are not entirely discrete stages. You should also note that the section on gathering information assumes that you have a general familiarity with the methods and materials of legal research. It also assumes access to a basic legal research text. Some are recommended at the end of this chapter.

A. GATHERING INFORMATION

Just as there is no one infallible strategy for retrieving the case law and statutory authorities that govern a client's problem, so there is no one surefire way to research your seminar paper or law review article. An effective strategy is always the function of two variables: your subject matter and your own personal style. There are, however, some sound general principles: stay current, reach out and ask someone, and start with secondary authority. In addition, there is one absolute rule: be thorough.

1. Be Thorough

The goal of your scholarly research is to develop and document a new and plausible thesis about some aspect of the law. Thus, your "mostly research" stage is not complete until you are *certain* that no one has said precisely what you want to say, and until you can demonstrate your thesis convincingly against a carefully documented background. Until you reach this stage, you should not begin your first full draft. Of course, it may happen that in the course of writing this draft, ideas will surface that send you back to the library, but this writing stage of research will almost always be purely supplemental.

It is easy to urge thoroughness, but difficult to explain how the researcher knows how much research is enough. Of course, so long as you continue to find new materials that are relevant, you must continue. But when you find the same materials no matter where you look, you can be fairly certain that the circle is closing. For instance, when online full-text searches, *Shepard's*, *American Law Reports* (A.L.R.) annotations, and key number searches have retrieved the same cases, it is respectable to quit; when more and more effort yields less and less result, it is time to wind down the search.

You should remember, however, that as with practice-oriented research, a search of just one source or a search that uses just one method is *never* sufficient, no matter how successful in itself. For example, online full-text searches can be particularly treacherous in this respect. Although a good WESTLAW query or LEXIS search —whether terms-and-connectors or natural language—will retrieve *only* materials on point, no search or query can ever be guaranteed to find *all* of the relevant documents. By the same token, print index searches are fallible because the indexers' categorization may be flawed or of little use for your purposes.

A careful search of legal periodicals is of course crucial to any scholarly enterprise, not least of all to ensure that your paper has not been "pre-empted" by another writer's work. One good way to gauge the thoroughness of your search of legal periodicals is to browse through the footnotes of the articles you have found. When you no longer find relevant new articles cited, you may be ready to move on, especially if you have found some very recent articles.

You should bear in mind, however, that a thorough search of legal periodicals is not only one of the most crucial, but also one of the most arduous and time-consuming of research tasks. There are two main indexes, the *Index to Legal Periodicals* (I.L.P.) and *Current Law Index* (C.L.I.). Both are available in print, online, and on CD-ROM, and both are published monthly and cumulated quarterly and annually. But they have different coverage—C.L.I. indexes more periodicals than the I.L.P., while the I.L.P. goes back much farther, to 1908—and they use quite different headings. It is often necessary to search under a number of headings in each. In addition, a non-cumulating index, the *Current Index to Legal Periodicals*, (C.I.L.P.) appears weekly and uses yet a third system of headings! Finally, some legal periodicals are available online and on CD-ROM, and thus articles on particular topics may be retrieved using full-text searches or queries, a resource which provides a valuable supplement to category-bound index searches. However, since not all legal periodicals are currently available in this format, and since all full-text searches are fallible, painstaking search of the several indexes is still a necessity.

If you attempt to do all of your periodical research in one sitting, or even in one day, you may well burn out, however, and compromise the thoroughness of your research. As suggested above, it is always a good idea to vary your research tasks—but when consulting indexes, variety is a real necessity. For instance, when you find a reference to an article that interests you, note down where you left off your index search, find the article, and read it. Besides relieving the tedium, alternating pure search with serious reading can suggest fruitful new directions for the search itself.

Finally, in order to be thorough, you must be patient. The literature of the law is vast; reported decisions number in the millions. If you bog down, just take a break, ask for help, and persevere.

2. *Stay Current*

Most scholarly writing in the law is concerned with current trends, developments, and controversies. It is thus usually a good idea to look for the most recent article or case first. In this respect, looseleaf services (whether *The United States Law Week* or the more specialized services like the *Criminal Law Reporter* or *Products Liability Reports*), the *Current Index to Legal Periodicals*, and WESTLAW's *Shepard's Preview* (which lists the most recent citing cases published in West's National Reporter System advance sheets), are particularly good places for the scholarly researcher to begin. By the same token, some sources are inappropriate starting places. In general, digests and encyclopedias are bad places to begin, because their indexes were formulated a long time ago and do not always adequately describe the current shape of the law. Finally, your research should be current in the sense of being as thoroughly up to date as you can make it.

3. *Reach Out and Ask Someone*

The best way to find that leading case or that seminal article is often just to ask. The experienced researcher's first question is "Who would have reason to know about this?" Professors are a good source of start-up information, and so are practitioners. Most reported decisions include the name of the attorneys who litigated the case. A telephone call to one or both attorneys can be a very fruitful first step, especially if you are writing a casenote. Since most people respond favorably to sincere expressions of interest in their work, you may well find yourself rewarded by a discussion of the case and copies of the briefs.

Librarians are also great sources of information. In this information age, the methods and materials of legal research are supplemented constantly. Librarians are in touch with the latest technology and know what is available in your particular library and how to get what is not. If you are stumped, and your research text does not help, ask a librarian, nicely. Finally, both LEXIS and WESTLAW have "800" numbers staffed by experts in online research.

4. Start with Secondary Sources

An experienced researcher's first step is always to see whether someone else has already compiled and summarized the information. When personal contacts do not find that expert, the next logical step is to consult secondary sources. Using digests or online full-text searches in a quest for primary sources is normally the last resort.

In the first year of law school, legal research instruction often focuses on finding case law and statutes in reporters and codes, using digests, Shepard's, and the online services. This focus is appropriate to the first year, first of all because it recognizes that reporters and codes are indeed where the law lives. The first-year emphasis on unmediated access to primary sources is also a practical necessity, because researching through digests, Shepard's, and full-text searches is a complex process unique to the law. In contrast, access to secondary sources—largely through indexes—is relatively simple once you gain some familiarity with the language of the law.

Yet the emphasis on primary sources has an unfortunate result: approaching their first scholarly research, students often waste precious time and enthusiasm by not starting with secondary sources, which can provide helpful overviews of the subject, a range of ideas about it, and compilations of primary sources. *Which* secondary source you begin with will depend on your subject, and also on your own preference. Some researchers look first to a looseleaf service for an up-to-the-minute capsule report; others look to treatises or to A.L.R. for objective overviews and up-dated case compilations; still others look to law reviews for the intellectual stimulation provided by a broad spectrum of opinion. Law review articles are also a good source of case compilations—but since law reviews are not updated, you may have to find the most recent cases yourself.

Although secondary sources are almost always the best places to gain an overview of a subject and begin the compilation of primary sources, you are never exempted from the duty to read and evaluate primary sources for yourself. It is tempting, but fatal to a scholar's mandate, to go along with a commentator's analysis rather than forming your own views from a careful consideration of the evidence. Bear in mind that the writers and compilers of secondary sources are human too, and thus biased and fallible. Maintain your independence of judgment and always test compilations to be sure that no relevant document escaped the compiler.

There is just one general exception to the rule that secondary sources are the best place to begin: if you are writing a casenote or a seminar paper that focuses on one case, you should begin by reading it and any lower court opinions and then finding and reading critically every authority cited in your case, whether binding or persuasive, primary or secondary. The direction of your research will inevitably become clear from close study of your case and all of the authority cited by the court—indeed, the court's use of precedent may well provide you with a thesis. Moreover, by starting this way, and recording your own reactions as you read, you may be better able to resist easy acquiescence to the views of other writers.

When your subject is interdisciplinary or otherwise requires you to do research in other fields, you will be using secondary sources almost exclusively. If personal contacts do not provide a productive starting place, two excellent all-purpose research guides are certain to help. Both of the following are available in libraries and (in paperback) in bookstores.

- *Finding Facts Fast*, by Alden Todd, published by Ten Speed Press
- *Find It Fast*, by Robert I. Berkman, published by Harper Collins

Another useful text is *Reference Books: A Brief Guide*, published by the Enoch Pratt Free Library in Baltimore.

In general, periodical indexes tend to be a good place to start. The *Index to Periodical Articles Related to Law* (I.P.A.R.L.) is one of the best. There are two other major sources of information about virtually every aspect of our society that professional researchers rely on: the state and federal governments and various trade, professional, and other special-interest organizations. The key, again, is the question, "Who would need to know?" Among many useful government publications, two stand out. The *United States*

Government Organization Manual, issued annually, describes the mandate of every government agency and may be able to help you find an expert on your subject. The *Statistical Abstract of the United States*, published annually since 1879, is a true mega-source of data gathered by government and private entities about a vast variety of subjects, including demography, economics, and commerce. In addition, the *Encyclopedia of Associations*, published by the Gale Research Company and updated every two years, is another excellent way to locate both experts and expertly compiled information. Finally, the two major online news and information services, WESTLAW's DIALOG and Mead Data Central's NEXIS provide access to a considerable archive of fairly recent newspapers, trade journals, and magazines. Full-text search techniques are like those used on WESTLAW and LEXIS. The libraries and databases of these services are frequently supplemented; you should always check their coverage before using them.

B. ASSIMILATING INFORMATION

Research, no matter how exhaustive, is useless unless you make it your own by critical reading, careful and methodical note-taking, and logical organization of your notes. Chapter Two discusses techniques of close and critical reading as an aid to the process of inspiration. Yet once you have found and researched your thesis, those same techniques will help you make intelligent and original use of the fruits of the research stage. Although materials that are tangential or clearly cumulative or duplicative may be skimmed or browsed, any text with a real bearing on your thesis, or which provides essential background, must be read with a critical eye and more than once.

You should almost never read without writing. Indeed, experienced writers often feel uncomfortable reading except pen-in-hand, whether taking notes or scribbling marginal comments. Highlighters do not count, because you cannot write down your ideas with them. They are enemies of critical thought, allies of summary and paraphrase.

Whether you write by hand or wordprocess your notes, there are a few important rules. These are rules that no researcher is ever able to observe all of the time. However, all researchers have reason to regret their lapses, which are inevitably self-punished by last-minute panic and duplicated effort.

The first rule is "be comprehensive." When you are reading a case or article that is central to your analysis, or that provides crucial background, take very thorough notes. Indeed, it is a good idea to indicate in your notes whether the text is important or incidental. Notations like "superficial analysis - skimmed" or "first article to discuss rights of domestic partners," or even "consulted - irrelevant" can be invaluable. (Every scholarly writer has had the experience of rushing out at the last minute to consult a case or article only to discover it was one she read two months earlier and discarded as irrelevant, but neglected to write down that fact in her notes.)

Your notes on important sources should ideally be so complete, and quote so accurately, that you can write your first draft without recourse to the original. In particular, you can save yourself last-minute anguish by including complete citation and bibliographical information in correct Bluebook form in your notes. (Of course, checking for accuracy is an important part of the polishing process.) If, being human, you falter in your note-taking zeal, you can safely admit it to your notes: "skimmed pp. 125-183, need better notes." Because good notes of important sources are not just paraphrase, but include generous portions of quotation and reflection, index cards are *not* very helpful: even the large ones may be too small for comprehensive note-taking. Notebooks or yellow pads perforated at top or sides are useful: you can take notes on a variety of sources, then tear off the pages and file them. Three-ring binders are very helpful here. You might begin by filing your notes according to the *type* of source: e.g. judicial opinions, law review articles, treatises. As you begin to see patterns and basic ideas emerging, you could put stick-on notes on the pages to make retrieval easier. You could also then refile your notes by issue. Finally, as your ideas become still more focused, you could use stick-ons again and refile again.

Good notes not only include your own reactions to the text, but also distinguish absolutely clearly between your ideas and what you have read. You might adopt the reading-journal style described in Chapter Two, Part B(2), using one side of the page for the author's ideas or the court's reasoning and one side for your own thoughts. Or you might simply preface your own reflections by your initials. In any event, meticulous distinction between self and text will ensure that the ideas put forward as your own are indeed your own and that sources are properly credited.

Finally, your comprehensive and carefully attributed notes will be of limited use unless you organize them. The best organization tracks your thesis. You should develop your own categories from the moment your thesis begins to take shape —assigning primary and secondary sources to issues, noting where you might want to use that source. Of course, you may need to revise or fine-tune as your ideas take a more definite shape.

REFERENCES FOR FURTHER READING

ROBERT I. BERKMAN, FIND IT FAST, Harper Collins (1990).

MORRIS L. COHEN, & ROBERT C. BERRING, HOW TO FIND THE LAW, West (9th ed. 1993); FINDING THE LAW, West (9th ed. 1993).

CHRISTINA L. KUNZ, DEBORAH A. SCHMEDEMANN, ANN L. BATESON, MATTHEW P. DOWNS, & C. PETER ERLINDER, THE PROCESS OF LEGAL RESEARCH, Little, Brown & Co. (3rd ed. 1992).

ALDEN TODD, FINDING FACTS FAST, Ten Speed Press (1979).

CHAPTER FOUR

THE WRITING PROCESS: GETTING IT DOWN ON PAPER

"Those who plan to relax until their creative inspiration seizes them may have a long uninterrupted rest."

- John R. Hayes

After choosing a subject and developing a thesis, the hardest part of any writing project is beginning it. Red Smith, a well-known sports writer, reportedly said: "Writing? Nothing to it. Just sit down at your typewriter and open a vein." Although many can appreciate this sentiment, such dire strategies have an untoward finality.

Beginning is hard because, even if we have some idea of what we want to say before we start, our thoughts are often in rich disarray. The order in which information is retrieved and ideas occur is all too often not a logical order. Somehow we must wrest an outline out of our research and brainstorming activities and impose order on what is anarchy. Sometimes this order does not come until we have meandered through several drafts, during which process we find out what we actually know and think about a subject. Some writers, however, are made anxious by this freewheeling process and find they cannot write at all without some kind of outline. These writers may panic if their research and prewriting thinking do not crystalize into an organizational scheme. Still other writers have such high standards that they discard any draft is not logically organized, thoroughly and creatively argued, and fluidly written. But because the details—the "nitty gritty"—of most arguments emerge only in the writing of them, because many points need refining as we realize logic or evidence does not fully bear them out, such perfectionists are likely to feel doomed early on.

Nonetheless, the early stages of writing become a lot more bearable if we lower our expectations for rough drafts—if we accept that writing is a time-consuming process and that papers, like people, mature slowly. The thing to keep in mind is that your first task is to get your ideas out on the table, that is to say, down on paper. Your second task, fleshing out those ideas and putting them in an order and prose your reader will find logical and compelling, is something you can work toward. Organization and readability can be achieved in stages and through a variety of tactics and techniques. This chapter and the next will describe some of those tactics and techniques.

A. WORKING TOWARD AN OUTLINE

If you have a good grasp on your thesis and the types of arguments you plan to make, you may find it easy and profitable to play with the traditional organizational structure of casenotes and comments and with classic organizational paradigms. (See Part B.) Simple adaptation of organizational schemes will not work for you, however, if you are at an earlier stage—still forging new concepts, synthesizing material, or weeding primary ideas from secondary ideas. Instead you may need to build slowly to an outline, by writing a "dump" or "zero" draft, making lists, or drawing diagrams. Sometimes it is helpful to use all three techniques.

1. Freewriting "Dump" or "Zero" Drafts

In Chapter Two, we recommended freewriting as a method for generating theses through uncensored but sustained free-association on a topic. Many writers also regard freewriting as a good way to generate an outline and first draft. This kind of freewriting is often called a "dump" draft[1] or "zero" draft[2] (as opposed to a first draft) because it remains that kind of private, exploratory, expressive writing that we would be reluctant to submit to another's scrutiny.

Dump or zero drafts require you to dump on the page every thought you have about your thesis and topic without regard for order, grammar, or brilliance. You can free-associate, summarize material, quote phrases you remember, make lists. Your freewriting might look something like the one below, a student's meditations on *Doe v. Taylor*,[3] a case in which the Fifth Circuit Court of Appeals ruled that the state had an affirmative duty to protect a fifteen-year-old public-school student from sexual molestation by her teacher because compulsory school attendance laws create a special relationship by giving the school functional custody of the student.

Freewriting

Case is important because it departs from DeShaney [State has no constitutional duty to protect child from abuse by father after it received reports of abuse when child not in its custody] and embraces a custody analysis.

To a feminist, important because imposes liability for sexual abuse and harassment in schools. What are the implications given the plaintiff is a young woman, a high school student...not a child?

Has social pressure dictated the decision? Outrage over DeShaney. Also sexual harassment is a hot topic...Anita Hill. Plus backlash over reproductive rights for the less empowered.

Or is Doe premised on statutory rape assumptions? The chastity & innocence of young women. Or just of a child, not a young woman. In an attempt to right the wrong of DeShaney, does Doe fail because it is a pervasive intrusion into the lives of H.S. students? Was this an affair or an assault?

What is interesting to me in Doe is the concept of the state protecting those incapable of protecting themselves b/c a custodial relationship exists. This is a 15-year-old young woman. Is she incapable? Is the situation out of her control? What are we protecting her from? sex? sexual harassment? Consequences of rejecting a teacher? The denial of a sound educational environment? Bodily integrity? The imagery in Doe conjures up five-year-olds and the mentally retarded being tied up in chairs and fondled. It seems different here, given that Jane snuck out of the house to meet her "molester" and lied to protect him—but the result is the same, being that the school has a duty to protect five-year-olds, as well as the fifteen-year-olds having sex with the biology teacher.

One law review article says that a student's consent to a sexual relationship with a teacher is inherently suspect and legally ineffective because of the coercive power imbalance. Thus age or maturity of a student is not determinative. Do I believe this? Believe in the presumption of coercion? Is this better than the custody analysis?

The helplessness analysis has backfired in women's law before.
- battered women and learned helplessness
- rape   :
                 :   but women are sexual
                 :   actors, not only victims
- pornography   :

> Here too the helplessness analysis has pitfalls...women
> have to show helplessness, a brassy adolescent should not
> be denied protection from sexual harassment because
> sexually active.
>
> Court didn't discuss power imbalance. What are
> the harmful effects? To education? To emotional
> welfare? To relations with peers? Taboo topics...both
> the young and their sexuality and student/teacher affairs.
>
> I need to find a way to grant relief, despite a
> young woman's brazen behavior, and not b/c parents
> don't want kids to have sex until marriage, or b/c she is
> unable to help herself or is in school custody. Need
> grounds that link the problems of fourteen-year-olds to
> women experiencing gender subordination in daily life.
> Is Meritor's test [whether the defendant's sexual conduct
> toward the plaintiff created a "hostile environment"]
> relevant to Doe's situation? Is it a more empowering
> analysis?

When your freewriting is finished, you can try to pull an outline out of the draft, or if you prefer, you can undertake the more focused types of freewriting discussed in Chapter Two in an effort to produce actual text for the first draft.

To pull an outline out of a dump draft, you must first comb through the draft spotting and relating points: highlight all ideas that seem profitable, delete the ideas that appear irrelevant, and cross-reference recurring and related themes. When we examine the freewriting we have provided above, for example, we notice that it opens with a misleadingly upbeat initial reaction to the *Doe* decision based on the writer's approval of the result. Yet closer scrutiny makes it clear that the dump draft contains several criticisms of the decision and even a criticism of the writer's own criticism.

> - Liability based on functional custody may be appropriate
> for a grade school child, but a high school student can, at
> least up to a point, protect herself...a distinction may be
> needed.
> - High school students may well be sexually active...not
> necessarily passive, not always victims.
> - Feminist legal thinking is turning against legal theories
> based on helplessness.
> - Functional custody seems posited on helplessness.
> - Student and teacher might be having a love affair...Or
> is the power imbalance inherently coercive?

Having listed these thoughts, the writer's next step is to try some provisional orderings. Group related points; articulate headings, categories, or unifying principles that encompass details; separate primary and secondary ideas; play with hierarchical orders. In the end, make sure that each division is based on a single principle, that the sum of the parts equals a whole, and that each part is mutually exclusive. Such an exercise resulted in the following tentative outline.

I.   Functional custody provides inappropriate grounds for holding school districts liable for sexual molestation under the due process clause because courts must create law that is responsive to women's true experiences.

    A.   Functional custody is a bright line test. Liability is posited on characterization of young women as passive and dependent.

    B.   The sexuality of high school students is too complex for a bright line rule.

    C.   Moreover, the functional custody standard limits understanding of the nature and impact of sexual harassment of students on teachers.

        1.   It focuses on sexual contact alone.

        2.   It is insensitive to how the imbalance of power affects other aspects of a teenager's life—like her education and social welfare.

As seen above, sustained freewriting can thus help you generate an outline. It is also a way to produce actual text. Sometimes, simply by deleting digressions and looping together related points, actual paragraphs emerge. More often, text is generated through freewriting focused on a particular topic. Begin by summarizing in a couple of sentences one of the main ideas in your initial freewriting. Then examine that idea by working up first impressions, embarking on further free association, writing from varying points of view. You may, in the end, be able to work these more focused meditations into your first draft with only minor revision. In fact, you may find these passages have a greater immediacy and vividness than your prose normally exhibits. An authentic voice often emerges when you do not stop to censor yourself.[4]

2. *Using Charts and Diagrams*

Some writers find that it is hard to move directly from dump drafts to outlines. They find that graphic representations are helpful in gaining perspective on a body of material and are thus a necessary first step in the development of an outline. Case charts, cluster diagrams[5] and issue trees[6] are three types of visual representations.

a. *Case Charts*

Sometimes it is hard to get on top of your case law. You have read so much that it is hard to see patterns and trends. To get an overview, try diagramming your cases. List the cases down the margin. Parade the issues across the top. Then fill in the boxes. The chart below organizes the case law on a state's affirmative duty to protect students from sexual molestation and harassment.

Cases	Court	Due Process Violation Based On Breach of Affirmative Duty to Protect?	State Deprivation of Liberty to Act Own Behalf?	Abuse by Private or State Actor?	State Knowledge of Danger?
DeShaney v. Winnebago (1989)	U.S. Sup. Ct.	No	No	Private (father)	Yes
Stoneking v. Bradford (1990)	3rd Cir.	Yes	Yes functional custody [FC] based on Compulsory Attendance Law [CAL]	State (Teacher)	?
Doe v. Taylor (1992)	5th Cir.	Yes	Yes FC = CAL	State (Teacher)	Yes
Yvonne L. v. New Mexico (1992)	10th Cir.	Yes	Yes state ordered foster care	Private	?
Pagana v. Massapequa (1989)	2nd Cir.	Yes	Yes FC = CAL	Private (Other student)	?

b. Cluster Diagrams

At times, you may have trouble relating facts to legal issues. Try creating a cluster diagram. Write down some ideas and details and draw lines attaching details to main ideas.

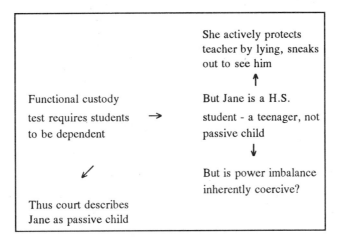

c. Issue Trees

Once you have a sense of how points relate to each other, you can try drawing an issue tree. Put a primary idea—a broad, inclusive point—at the top of your tree and work down to subpoints. You may find you need to create subheadings that relate and encompass specific details. You may also find some subpoints are actually new issues, separate branches requiring separate discussions.

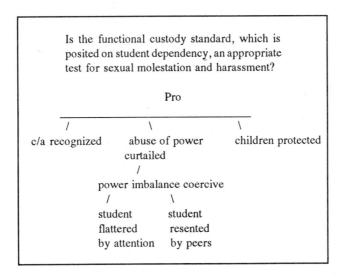

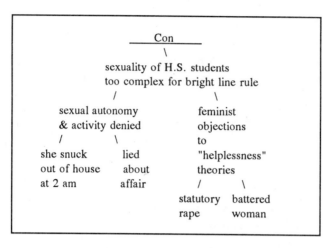

This working tree can then be revised into a hierarchical outline.

I.   The result in <u>Doe v. Taylor</u> is correct, but the functional custody test is inappropriate.

A.   The decision will have some positive effects on sexual harassment and sexual molestation claims.

1. Cause of action for harassment in schools recognized for the first time.

2. School children are protected.

3. Abuse of power is curtailed.

B.   But the decision may have unforeseen negative effects on women's law.

1. The sexual autonomy of high school students is denied.

2. The myth of women's passivity and victimization is continued.

3. The standard is objectionable for the same reasons some feminists reject statutory rape statutes or "learned helplessness" in the Battered Woman's Syndrome defense.

B. CREATING AN OUTLINE

As we said earlier, once you have a grasp on your thesis and arguments, you can turn to traditional organizational schemes to help you order your material. Scholarly articles do not always need to be organized from scratch. Like the boilerplate of pleadings, leases, contracts, or wills, casenotes and comments have a traditional structure that provides at least a provisional framework for organizing and sorting some of your material. Moreover, each part of the note or comment has a purpose that further informs its content and organization. Finally, there are recognized organizational paradigms—basic patterns of reasoning— that can aid in organizing the background or analysis section.

1. *Adapting the Traditional Casenote or Comment Outline*

The structure of a casenote, a comment, or a seminar paper is essentially the same. At a minimum, all three move from an introduction through background and analysis sections to a conclusion. Only the section called "Statement of the Case" is peculiar to the casenote. Thus, with some modification, law review articles and seminar papers tend to be modelled on the following outline.

Introduction
1. Introduce and note why the topic is important.
2. Briefly summarize necessary background information.
3. State your thesis.
4. Convey your organization of the paper.

Background

1. Describe the genesis of the subject.
2. Describe the changes that have occurred during its development.
3. Explain the reasons for the changes.
4. Describe where things are now. (You may also want to indicate the reasons for further change.)

Statement of the Case (casenote)

1. Include the relevant facts.
2. Include the procedural history.

3. Include the court's holding and reasoning at each level, as well as the reasoning of dissenting or concurring opinions.

Analysis

Large-scale organization

1. Discuss the major issues.
2. Separate issues and subissues.
3. Order issues logically.

Small-scale organization

4. Introduce and conclude on each issue.
5. Present your argument and rebut opposing arguments.
6. Use organizational paradigms where appropriate.

Conclusion

1. Restate thesis.
2. Summarize major points.

Although the outline provided above is a step toward a concise and logical exposition, you need not follow it rigorously. In the end, the issues raised by a particular case or topic should shape not only your analysis, but also your structure. Nonetheless, you may come up with a useful provisional outline if you try plugging the specific content of your topic into this structure. Be sure that your outline is substantive; an outline consisting of words and phrases is rarely helpful. A good outline asserts your ideas, usually in full (if unpolished) sentences.

2. Using Paradigms

In shaping your analysis, you may want to borrow from established organizational paradigms when your arguments correspond naturally with them. You may find it helpful to use a general outline in conjunction with basic paradigms.

Comparative paradigms arise when you need to justify one choice among competing alternatives and interests. A topic that involves, for example, balancing litigants' competing interests or choosing among different policies or jurisdictional approaches lends itself to one of two comparative paradigms.

The *alternating pattern* examines each point in terms of the alternatives.

> Thesis Statement
>> Point One
>>> Alternative A
>>> Alternative B
>> Point Two
>>> Alternative A
>>> Alternative B
>> Point Three
>>> Alternative A
>>> Alternative B
> Comparison and Evaluation of the Alternatives

The *divided pattern* is organized around the alternatives rather than the points.

> Thesis Statement
>> Alternative A
>>> Point One
>>> Point Two
>>> Point Three
>> Alternative B
>>> Point One
>>> Point Two
>>> Point Three
> Comparison and Evaluation of Alternatives

A divided pattern similar to the one above was used in a law review article on the results of two surveys on workable definitions of pornography.[7]

```
    I. The First Survey on Three Definitions of Pornography
         A. Vagueness
         B. Overbreadth and Underbreadth
         C. Demographic Breakdown of Responses
   II. The Second Survey on Three Definitions of Pornography
         A. Vagueness
         B. Overbreadth and Underbreadth
         C. Demographic Breakdown of Responses
```

Had the author wished, he could have used the alternating pattern, as follows.

```
    I. Vagueness
         A. The First Survey
         B. The Second Survey
   II. Overbreadth and Underbreadth
         A. The First Survey
         B. The Second Survey
  III. Demographic Breakdown
         A. The First Survey
         B. The Second Survey
```

In deciding whether to use a divided or alternating pattern, you should be aware that each of these patterns has its own advantages and disadvantages. The alternating pattern provides for a clear point-by-point assessment of the alternatives, but the larger picture may recede into the background. Thus the alternating pattern often begins or ends with an overview. The divided pattern provides the reader with a good grasp of each alternative but a point-by-point assessment is harder. Thus, the writer using the divided pattern would be wise to refer back to the first discussion when she gets to the second, or to provide a comparative overview after each alternative has been discussed.

The paradigm most common in legal scholarship is the *problem-solution pattern*. This paradigm is useful if, for example, you have identified a problem that you think could be solved by a new rule, exception, or modification.

- Identify and explain problem
- Announce and explain solution
- Explain how and why solution solves problem

This paradigm is followed in the analysis section of a law review article on Establishment Clause adjudication.[8]

IV. Disjuncture Between Theory and Law: Inability of Existing Establishment Clause Tests to Ensure Religious Liberty **[The Problem]**
- A. The *Lemon* Test: The Impossibility of Strict Neutrality
  - 1. The Effect Prong of the *Lemon* Test
  - 2. *Lemon* Test as a Threat to Religious Liberty
- B. The Endorsement Test: The Unfulfilled Promise of Symbolic Neutrality
  - 1. Dimensions of Endorsement Test: *Lynch v. Donnelly*
  - 2. Deficiencies in the Endorsement Test
    - a. Terminology Without Content: Insurmountable Barrier to Implementation
    - b. Irrelevance and Incompatibility: Failure of the Endorsement Test to Guard Individual Religious Liberty

V. Protecting Individual Religious Liberty: A Coercion-Based Test **[The Solution]**
- A. The Significance of Coercion to the Drafters of the First Amendment and to Supreme Court Justices
- B. Previous Attempts to Formulate a Coercion Test
- C. The Proposed Test
  - 1. Defining Coercive Effect
  - 2. Determining when the Coercive Effect Is Impermissible

VI. Applications of the Coercion Test **[Demonstration of how Solution Solves Problem]**
- A. Economic Aid to Religion
  - 1. Educational Setting: Aid to Parochial Schools
  - 2. Noneducational Setting
- B. Noneconomic Aid to Religion
  - 1. Educational Settings: Religion in the Public Schools
  - 2. Noneducational Setting

Sometimes you will need to use a *cause and effect pattern*. You must use this pattern to explain the evolution of law, as in the background section, or to predict developments, as in the analysis section.

- Effect [status quo or result] is announced
- Possible causes announced
- Evidence presented on how causes lead to the effect

Sometimes one type of organizational paradigm becomes embedded in another and, as they do, your outline grows more complex. For example, you may need to use a comparative pattern within a problem-solution paradigm to show why one solution is better than another, or, as below, you may need to embed cause and effect in a problem-solution paradigm.[9]

I.   Introduction
II.   Problem of Domestic Violence **[Problem] [Cause]**
        A.   Description of the Problem
        B.   Psychology of the Battered Family
                1.   Victims
                2.   Abusers
                3.   Children
III.   Child Custody Decisionmaking **[Background]**
IV.   State Response **[Effect]**
        A.   Modifications to the Statutory Joint Custody Standard
        B.   Modifications to Best Interest of the Child Statutes
        C.   Court Decisions
                1.   Courts Dismissing Domestic Violence
                2.   Courts Influenced by Domestic Violence
                        a.   Sole Custody
                        b.   Joint Custody Decisions
                        c.   Cases in Which One Parent
                                Has Killed the Other
        D.   Summary
V.   Overcoming Myths About Domestic Violence **[Explanation of How Causes Led to Effect]**
        A.   Myths About Domestic Violence **[Problem]**
        B.   Overcoming Myths **[Solution]**
VI.   Integrating Domestic Violence Into Child Custody Decisions **[Solution]**
        A.   Recast Assumptions Concerning Fitness of the Natural Parents
        B.   Admit Evidence of Abuse
        C.   Visitation
        D.   Train Judges
        E.   Consider Domestic Violence in Custody and Visitation Modifications
VII.   Conclusion

C. WRITING THE DRAFT

*"The last thing one discovers in writing a
book is what to put first."*
- Blaise Pascal

The techniques we have described so far are primarily
directed to helping you outline your paper. Although some writers
never outline, most would probably admit that it is easier to write
with an outline than without one. If you have already worked out the
large-scale organization of your piece, you do not have to worry
about where to go next. This frees you to concentrate more fully on
the particulars of the moment, on documenting and wording your
contentions.

Once you are ready to sit down and write a full draft, here is
another piece of advice: Begin anywhere. Many people labor under
the misconception that the right way to write is to begin at the
beginning, with the introduction, and to move sequentially through to
the conclusion. But there is no real reason to write a document in the
order you must eventually present it.   In fact, introductions are
notoriously difficult to write cold. A moment's reflection makes it
obvious that a clear statement of your thesis and organization may be
easier to write after the fact than before. Indeed, the habit of writing
a draft straight through, without rewriting the introduction, may
explain why the theses of so many articles are more clearly stated in
the conclusion than in the introduction.

It is often helpful to write in the order of ease.   Is
summarizing a decision the easiest thing to do? Write it first. Are
you clearer about one point than another? Start there. Not only does
your confidence build as you document grows, but a lot of subliminal
thinking—a lot of sorting, discarding, and combining—may be
occurring as you work on other sections. When you finally get to the
thorniest argument, you may find yourself better prepared to handle
it. In fact, you may get ideas for that thorny section as you are
working on something else. If you do, take the time to scribble them
down; otherwise you may lose them. Once you have written enough
to jog your memory, return to the section you have been working on.

One problem with "order of ease" writing is that it tends to
suffer from poor transitions. When you write out of order, or if you
write without an outline, you must take special care to review your
work with an eye to organization and smooth, logical connections.

Outline your draft after it is done and examine its structure for logical development.

But whether you work straight through from introduction to conclusion or work in order of ease, try to schedule your work so that you can work without interruptions of more than a day or two. Picking up the cold trail of your ideas can be a lengthy and anxiety-inducing process. One good tip, usually attributed to Ernest Hemingway, is to stop writing when you know what you are going to say next, not when you are stumped. This will make it easier to begin when you next start writing. But before you stop, jot down your thoughts about what to do next, or you may lose them.

Finally, if you become bent on perfecting a particular passage and time is running out, try "invisible" writing. When rewriting is an evasion blocking your progress, turn off your computer screen and forge ahead. Once your head is full of new ideas for the next section, you can turn the screen back on. Polishing your prose is a necessary *last* step in the writing process. Do not let it inhibit the drafting stage.

All the techniques we have discussed in this chapter are meant to produce a first full draft. A first full draft differs from a zero draft, dump draft, or rough draft in its greater organization, development, and clarity of purpose. A first full draft has all the requisite parts of a paper, including footnotes, and all the main arguments. It is a document that needs to be revised and perfected, not a document that needs to be created. First full drafts are often shorter than your finished paper—or longer. If the draft is short, it may be because it needs further documentation and explication. You may also need to add introductions and conclusions to each section, as well as transitions. If the draft is very long, it may be because it is repetitive or wordy. There may be confusing digressions. Nonetheless, in some form, all your ideas have been articulated. The paper contains enough information and enough structure that, after a break, both you and an outside reader can see what work remains to be done.

NOTES

1.   MARY B. RAY & BARBARA J. COX, BEYOND THE BASICS: A TEXT FOR ADVANCED LEGAL WRITING 12 (1991).

2.   Jill N. Burkland & Bruce T. Petersen, *An Integrative Approach to Research: Theory and Practice*, in CONVERGENCES: TRANSACTIONS IN READING AND WRITING 199 (Bruce T. Petersen, ed., 1986).

3.   975 F.2d 137 (5th Cir. 1992).

4.   FREDERIC G. GALE & JOSEPH M. MOXLEY, HOW TO WRITE THE WINNING BRIEF 16 (1992).

5.   *See id*. at 19-20; LAUREL C. OATES, ANNE ENQUIST, & KELLY KUNSCH, THE LEGAL WRITING HANDBOOK 513-15 (1993).

6.   *See* LINDA FLOWER, PROBLEM-SOLVING STRATEGIES FOR WRITING, 87-94 (1981); GALE & MOXLEY, *supra* note 4, at 20-21.

7.   Adapted from James Lindgren, *Defining Pornography*, 141 U. PA. L. REV. 1153, 1154 (1993).

8.   Robert A. Holland, Comment, *A Theory of Establishment Clause Adjudication: Individualism, Social Contact, and the Significance of Coercion in Identifying Threats to Religious Liberty*, 80 CAL. L. REV. 1595, 1596-97 (1992).

9.   Naomi R. Cahn, *Civil Images of Battered Women: The Impact of Domestic Violence on Child Custody Decisions*, 44 VAND. L. REV. 1041 (1991).

CHAPTER FIVE

THE WRITING PROCESS: REVISING AND POLISHING

> *"The essence of editing [your own work] is easy come easy go. Unless you can really say to yourself, 'What the hell. There's plenty more where that came from, let's throw it away,' you can't really edit. You have to be a big spender."*
>
> *-Peter Elbow*

> *"What is written without effort is in general read without pleasure."*
>
> *-Samuel Johnson*

A. REVISION AND THE READER

When you have gone beyond the stage of outlines, charts, and zero drafts and completed your first full draft, the next step (after a proper celebration) is to read your work with a critical eye, to decide what revisions* are needed, and to make them. How extensively you revise and how many drafts you do will depend on your purpose, the

---

* We use "revision" generally to refer to any changes and improvements in a text. We also use it more specifically to refer to large-scale changes—content and overall organization. We use "polishing" to refer to smaller-scale revisions—the restructuring of individual paragraphs and sentences.

65

complexity of your subject-matter, and the level of skill and experience you bring to the project.

At no stage of the process is revision merely a matter of trying to say the same thing "better," however. Rather, revision is writing for the reader's eye, just as the "getting-it-down-on-paper" stage is writing for yourself, the discovery and memorialization of what you think. The goal of all revision is to convince your readers to see your subject as you do, in short, to *connect* with them. It is to that end that you will supplement or streamline your background material, reorganize your ideas in a more logical sequence, create or omit headings, add transitions, recast paragraphs to give them unity and cohesion, and polish your prose until it gleams.

Put another way, the revision process is governed by what composition theory calls the "rhetorical situation." Broadly defined, a rhetorical situation is the conjunction of three elements: *purpose*, *audience*, and various *constraints*, including the conventions of the genre and the skills of the persuader.[1] Sizing up the rhetorical situation—consciously or automatically—is a crucial moment in every writing project, even in the brainstorming stages. But it is above all when you revise that your particular rhetorical situation should inform all your efforts.

In order to convince your audience to see as you see, you must of course know your audience. The audience for legal scholarship is at once unitary and multiple: although it is drawn almost exclusively from the legal profession, the profession itself is diverse and becoming more so daily—composed as it is of litigators, state and federal judges and their clerks, legislators, prosecutors, public defenders, corporate counsel, law professors. Although your subject and thesis may tempt you to write exclusively for one of the micro audiences within the profession, this temptation should be resisted, unless you are writing for a specialized publication. The basic rhetorical situation of legal scholarship is idiosyncratic in that, although scholarly articles are largely read by specialists (contracts professors read articles on contracts and prosecutors read about criminal law), they are usually written for an audience of generalists that has in common only a law school education.

The specifics of revision discussed in the rest of this chapter are determined by the needs and expectations of an audience of law-school-educated readers and the conventions of scholarly writing. But *how much* revision is appropriate before submission of your draft will depend in part on how much you take your audience automatically into account in your first drafts. (Some experienced writers seem able to do this without sacrificing spontaneity or creativity.) The amount of revision you do before submission will also depend on the preference of your professor or editor. Some professors and editors believe that they can be most helpful to the writer if they read very early drafts because those versions track the writer's thought processes and often include significant insights that novice scholarly writers tend to censor when they revise. Other teachers and editors want a polished draft that takes their needs and expectations fully into account. For such readers, a first submitted draft means the most polished work that you can do on your own. Before you submit, be certain that you know which kind of draft your own particular first audience expects.

No matter how much or how little you do, you would do well to revise in the order of the sections that follow. Resist the temptation to tinker with wording before you have checked the content and organization of your draft. Polishing material that you may eventually discard or extensively reorganize can be a waste of precious time. (Yet, like all of the guidelines in our book, this is a signpost, not a hitching-post. There are times when rewriting just one sentence clarifies a writer's thinking so effectively that a better organization of the paper becomes immediately apparent. In the end, only you can decide what is the best way for *you* to proceed.)

B. GAINING PERSPECTIVE

The central difficulty of revision is that it requires you to be yourself and your reader at the same time, requires you both to know and not know what you know. When we read what we have written, we tend automatically to supply missing information and missing transitions. Ambiguity, vagueness, and over-generality often go unnoticed, because we know what we meant to say. Taking some time off between writing and revision is helpful, because what we wanted to say no longer interposes itself so solidly between ourselves and what we actually wrote. On the other hand, if we take too much time between writing and revision, the friendly ghost of our intentions may vanish entirely, leaving us wondering what on earth we were trying to say.

Having your draft look like a work in progress can also help you gain critical perspective. Word processors are wonderful tools, too wonderful sometimes: a word-processed first draft can look like a finished work, and it takes much determination on the writer's part to read it with a critical eye. Printing your draft triple-spaced or even quadruple-spaced and in a large font may help overcome such inhibitions.

Of course, you can revise entirely on the screen; some experienced writers work very successfully that way. One great advantage to on-screen revision is that you are never limited to what you can write between the lines. On the other hand, it is often easier to check content and organization on hard copy because you can more easily see the relation of the parts to the whole. Moreover, computer screens often encourage browsing and skimming, not close and critical reading. Words on a screen tend to seem impersonal, immutable somehow, even though we know we wrote them ourselves. But a scrawled on, crossed out, coffee-stained draft is *personal*—imperfect but full of possibility. You can carry it with you and use odds and ends of time to work on it.

C. REVISING: CONTENT

The obvious first step in the revision of scholarly writing is to be certain that you have provided your reader sufficient (but not suffocating) background material and that your analyses are appropriate and sufficiently developed (but not soporific). Early drafts often assume too much knowledge on the part of your audience. They are too specifically geared to a particular professor or editor, rather than for the audience identified earlier in this chapter—a law school graduate largely unfamiliar with your subject matter.

How much information that audience needs is difficult to gauge. In general, however, all but the very basics need to be supplied. You can assume, for instance, that your reader is familiar with fundamental structural concepts like judicial review and stare decisis. But, whether in footnote or in text, the substance of the law—no matter how obvious it seems—almost always needs to be articulated and documented. In requiring comprehensive documentation, legal scholarship is like scholarly writing in general. However, legal scholarship is much more densely documented than most scholarly writing in the humanities; this is one of its most frequently criticized aspects. (In connection with this discussion, you may want to read Part A of Chapter Six, on authority footnotes.)

For example, if you are writing a casenote about a recent state court decision concerning the propriety of warrantless searches of undeveloped land, you should note, however briefly, that the United States Constitution forbids unreasonable government searches of our houses and effects, and cite the Fourth Amendment in a footnote. Yet you would not ordinarily need to explain in your casenote that the Fourth Amendment was made applicable to the states by judicial "incorporation" into the Fourteenth Amendment, because this is an assumption fundamental to the contemporary legal culture.

Of course, the need for meticulous documentation does not mean that you should include irrelevant information. Nor does the existence of certain basic assumptions mean that there are no occasions for articulating and examining those assumptions. For instance, your casenote on warrantless searches of undeveloped land would not discuss the prerequisites for a valid warrant, nor would it discuss the exclusionary rule. But if your thesis is that the state court should have disagreed with the United States Supreme Court's interpretation of the Fourth Amendment and prohibited such searches, a discussion of the "incorporation" of the Fourth into the Fourteenth Amendment—ordinarily an unstated assumption—would be relevant because your thesis puts the relationship between the state and federal courts in issue.

Your descriptions of caselaw should also be tailored to your subject and thesis—they should not be case briefs. In the example given in Chapter Four, our student decided to write about a decision of the Fifth Circuit Court of Appeals holding that the state had a duty to protect a teenager from sexual molestation by her teacher because a compulsory education law gave the state "functional custody" of her and thus created a "special relationship." Our student's thesis was that although the result was proper, the court's "functional custody" rationale actually demeaned the victim. The paper would obviously have to include a discussion of the Supreme Court decision upon which the Fifth Circuit relied, *DeShaney v. Winnebago*.[2] There, the Supreme Court held that a state social services agency investigating a charge of child abuse was not responsible for the child's death at his father's hands, because absent a "special relationship" created by custody, the Due Process Clause does not create an affirmative duty to protect. The majority's opinion provoked a passionate dissent. Yet neither the horrific facts of *DeShaney* nor the reasoning of the dissent would be relevant to the student's paper: the Court's notion of a "special relationship" should be the only focus of her discussion of it, and any other aspects of *DeShaney* would be appropriate only in a textual footnote, if at all.

Although your thesis should largely dictate the amount and type of background information that you provide, you must be certain to provide enough information so that the reader can disagree as well as agree with you. For instance, if, like the author of one student note, you were writing about the proper role of *Miranda* warnings in prison, you would of course need to provide some background on *Miranda v. Arizona*—even though it is common knowledge among laypersons as well as lawyers that suspects in government custody must ordinarily be informed of their constitutional rights before being questioned.[3] If, like the writer, your thesis was that despite their undoubted custodial status, prison inmates do not invariably need to be "Mirandized" before questioning, your background section would obviously focus more on the Burger and Rehnquist Courts' pragmatic limitations on *Miranda* than on the policies that underlie *Miranda* itself. Yet if you ignored those policies, you would not be dealing candidly with your audience, one of a scholar's first responsibilities. By the same token, if your thesis was that *Miranda* warnings are *per se* required in prison, you would be obliged at the very least to document the practical arguments against such a rule.

Of course, checking the content of your draft requires you to take a long, hard look at your analysis, as well as the more objective and factual sections. Be sure that your position is consistent throughout: our ideas sometimes change in the course of writing a first draft. Be sure, too, that you are not begging the question—arguing from a debatable, but unargued premise—or generalizing from too little evidence. Finally, try to imagine *all* the arguments against your thesis. Then be certain you have dealt candidly with them. You cannot convince a reader to see as you see by sheer insistence that yours is the only true view.

When in doubt, it is better to provide too much background or too many examples rather than too little or too few, and better to flesh out your argument too solidly than too meagerly. As well as better serving the reader's needs, this rule of "more is more" can save you time and misery in the end. Write more rather than less while the information or reasoning is fresh in your mind, whether in the drafting or first revision stage. Trying to implement your editor's or professor's suggestion "I think you need some examples here" can be a major undertaking when you have been away from your material for weeks or even months. Editing down does not present the same problem.

Of course, "more is more" is not a license to go over the assigned page limit. If your paper or note starts to grow uncontrollably in revision, you are including irrelevant information and analysis, or your thesis is either not sufficiently focused or too ambitious for your page limit.

Finally, you may find that you can increase the reader-friendliness of your work by relegating information or arguments that are necessary, but not crucial, to footnotes. (You may also find, however, that material in a footnote fills an important gap in the text.)

D. REVISING: ORGANIZATION

> *"I sometimes think that writing is like driving sheep down the road. If there is a gate to the left or right, the readers will most certainly go into it."*
> *-C.S. Lewis*

Once you are certain that you have said all that you need to say to your reader and all that your reader needs to hear, the revision process can focus on organization, on connecting ideas and information in ways that make them easily accessible to the reader.

Human beings have very limited short-term memory, and as readers, we avoid total confusion only because we can put complex material into categories as we read and thus reduce the number of specifics to remember. We also put these categories into a hierarchical framework as we read: e.g. major idea, first minor constituent idea, second minor constituent idea, qualification of second minor constituent idea, etc. If the writer does not provide us with an unambiguous context, that is, a logical and clearly signposted hierarchical organization of the writer's material, two things happen to frustrate the writer's connection with us. First, we become confused and unreceptive. Second, we import or create our own context, one which may not be what the writer had in mind.

Thus, if you as the writer want your readers to see as you see, attention must be paid to your organization, both large-scale (the relation of the sections of your paper to each other) and small-scale (the relation of ideas within each section to each other). Attention must also be paid to your signposts, that is, the headings and introductions that announce the content of sections and sub-sections, and the transitions that make explicit the relationship between ideas.

1. *Large-scale Organization*

We said in Chapter One that the same basic four-part organization is appropriate to virtually all legal scholarship: introduction, background, analysis, and conclusion. Introductions and conclusions are traditionally very short, rarely more than a few pages, sometimes less than one. The introduction should state your thesis, providing just enough background to make it comprehensible to any law-school-educated reader. It must also include an explicit "roadmap" that provides your reader with a graphic itinerary—e.g., "Part I provides an overview of X doctrine, Part II discusses and evaluates recent decisions on X in state Y, and Part III argues that Z is the better view." (Note that the most usual practice is to leave the introduction and conclusion unnumbered and use roman numerals for the sections between.) A traditional conclusion restates your thesis and summarizes your analysis; ideally, it also inspires the reader to take up where you have left off.

Background and analysis often require more than one section each or may require division into subsections. In determining your sections, you will need to find categorizing principles that organize your material. For example, the necessary background might include both a historical overview and a summary of recent decisions. It might also include a discussion of your methodology. Similarly, your analysis might consist of a critique of existing approaches and your own proposed solution. Once you have conceptualized your sections, spend some time thinking about their order. Should methodology precede or follow the historical overview?

In general, these sections should be of roughly equal length. Very short and very long sections should usually prompt rethinking: a very short section might be just an aspect of the longer section, or it might need fleshing out. A disproportionately long section might more appropriately be two sections, or perhaps on the other hand it just needs trimming. In general, a major (i.e. roman numeral) section of a seminar paper or law review article should not be shorter than ten manuscript pages, and it may be much longer.

Be certain that the major sections of your paper or note are mutually exclusive—that is, that you have the right material, and only the right material, in the right place. Be sure that your background sections contain just that and do not segue imperceptibly into your analysis of that material. You should also check to see that your analysis does not contain afterthought background material: sometimes, as you draft your analysis, your thinking takes a new turn requiring more background material, and the easiest (but temporary) solution is simply to supply it as you go along. In the event that your particular topic and thesis dictate an organizational pattern in which alternative approaches are described and evaluated in the same section, the mutual-exclusivity principle can still be respected by putting information and opinion in separate *sub*-sections. In no event, however, should the reader be left wondering whether you are describing or evaluating.

2. *Small-scale Organization*

Being sure that the right material is in the right place is easier than the next step, checking your small-scale organization to see whether you present your material in clear and logical sequence. By its very nature, background information usually poses fewer organizational problems than does analysis. Much background is simple past-to-present narrative, and when you present a court's reasoning or another commentator's views, you work from a pre-existing organization, whether you choose to adopt, modify, or reject it. But your own thoughts are most difficult of all to organize.

One good way to check the organization of your analysis sections is to make a paragraph-by-paragraph topic outline. Be sure, however, that you are making an outline of what you wrote, not what you intended to write. Making the outline from the content of your topic sentences will avoid this temptation. If you find outlines uncongenial, try drawing an issue tree using the technique described in Chapter Four, Part A(2)(c), being certain, however, that your representation is realistic.

3. *Signposts*

Like justice, organization must not only be done, but also be seen to be done. Because anticipation is inherent in the reading process, you should give the reader explicit notice of the organization of your paper not only in the roadmap in the introduction, but also through the use of headings, section introductions and conclusions, topic sentences, and transitions. These signposts help get your ideas across by directing the reader's anticipation to your way of thinking. Of course, the number of signposts you use should be proportionate to the difficulty and complexity of your material; the trick is to keep your readers on the right road without insulting their intelligence.

a. Headings

Use headings to divide and subdivide the text of your paper or notes into appetizing and digestible portions. The main difficulties posed by headings are two: how many to use and how much substance to include in them.

With the exception of "Introduction" and "Conclusion," all of your headings should be substantive—and even your introduction and conclusion can have descriptive subtitles. Your headings should form a short substantive outline of your paper; some writers even print these heading-outlines at the beginning of their articles, a strategy you might consider if your subject and thesis are complex.   How descriptive your headings should be is a function of personal preference and the complexity or novelty of your material.   For instance, a writer urging a new theory of liability—negligent employment discrimination—under Title VII of the Civil Rights Act of 1964 understandably concluded that he needed detailed, didactic headings, and thus headed Part II of his article "The Supreme Court's Analysis of Employment Discrimination Incorporates Negligence Analysis and Invites the Development of an Independent Theory of Negligent Discrimination."[4]   On the other hand, more familiar material or less novel proposals would require less detail.   For instance, the author of the note on *Miranda* warnings in prison was able to use shorter, but still helpful headings, entitling his Part I, a background section, "*Miranda*, Prison Interrogation, and the Supreme Court."[5]

How many headings you use, that is, how finely you sub-divide your text, depends on the length and complexity of your work. Although headings help us hold onto our readers by guiding their anticipation, too many headings chop up the text, distracting and alienating the reader. In general, it is unwise to have more than two levels of subdivisions below the roman numeral level, and one level is usually sufficient. If you end up with subsections less than a page long, you are probably using too many headings. A good topic sentence directing your reader to the forthcoming material may be less disruptive and just as informative.

The effective headings of two student articles are reproduced below—the first is from a sixty-page comment, and the second is from a thirty-page casenote.

Rotating Japanese Managers in American
Subsidiaries of Japanese Firms: A
Challenge for American Employment
Discrimination Law[6]

I.   Introduction
II.   Allegations of Discrimination in Favor of Japanese Managers
        A.   Americans Excluded from Decisionmaking
                1.   Japanese-only meetings
                2.   Meetings conducted in Japanese
                3.   Information isolation
                4.   Japanese-only socializing
        B.   Titles Without Authority
        C.   Separate Career Paths for Japanese and American Staff
                1.   Glass ceiling for Americans
                2.   Americans bear burden of reductions in force
                3.   Americans replaced by less qualified Japanese
        D.   Summary
III.   Justifications and Explanations for Preferring Japanese Managers
        A.   Language
        B.   Business Practices
                1.   Training and experience
                2.   Management style
                3.   Criticism of business practices
                        rationale
        C.   Loyalty and Commitment
        D.   Trust and Comfort
        E.   Training of Japanese Staff
        F.   Racial Prejudice
        G.   Summary
IV.   Legal Analysis of Discrimination Cases Based
        on Preferences for Japanese Managers
        A.   Introduction
        B.   Arguments That Title VII Does Not Apply
                1.   Friendship, Commerce and Navigation Treaty
                2.   Citizenship discrimination
        C.   Introduction to Title VII Legal Theories
                1.   Disparate treatment
                2.   Disparate impact
        D.   Application of Title VII Legal Theories
                1.   Explanations that do not survive
                        Title VII
                2.   Possible business necessity defenses
        E.   Summary
V.   Conclusion

<u>EXAMPLE B</u>

Drug Testing: Can Privacy Interests Be
Protected Under the "Special Needs" Doctrine?[7]

Introduction
I.   Background
        A.   The Fourth Amendment
                1.   Steps in Fourth Amendment Analysis
                2.   The Rise of Reasonableness and Balancing
        B.   The Government's War on Drugs
II.   The Supreme Court Cases
        A.   *Skinner v. Railway Labor Executives Association*
                1.   Lower Court Proceedings
                2.   The Supreme Court Decision
                        a.   The Majority Opinion
                        b.   Justice Marshall's Dissent
        B.   *National Treasury Employees Union v. Von Raab*
                1.   Lower Court Proceedings
                2.   The Supreme Court Decision
                        a.   The Majority Opinion
                        b.   Justice Marshall's Dissent
                        c.   Justice Scalia's Dissent
III.   Analysis
        A.   "Special Needs": The Further Demise of
                Probable Cause
                1.   The Emergence of the "Special Needs"
                        Doctrine
                2.   Ramifications and Problems
        B.   Tipping the Balance in Favor of Privacy
                1.   Random Testing
                2.   Reasonable Suspicion Testing
        Conclusion

No matter how many or how few headings you use, be certain that each level (*i.e.*, Roman numerals, capital letters, etc.) requires more than one heading. Violation of the "no-A-without-B" rule suggests a flaw in the logic of your small-scale organization.

b. Section Introductions and Conclusions

"First you tell them what you're going to tell them, then you tell them, then you tell them what you told them."

-The Teacher's Credo

Just as important as headings are introductory paragraphs. Each section needs its own introduction, one that foreshadows the particular point or thesis to be made in that section and the arguments supporting the thesis. When a section is short and each point has been explicitly articulated, you may not need a concluding paragraph for that section. Where the section is long, however, readers find a brief recapitulation of the thesis and supporting arguments helpful. The purpose of the concluding paragraph is to draw together your points so that the meaning of that section is unmistakable.

c. *Topic Sentences and Transitions*

We can get home without reminding ourselves to turn left at the third traffic light or turn right off the elevator, but strangers need directions. In the same way, readers need explicit directions to guide them through our texts, especially when the road is long and twisting. Topic and transition sentences traditionally provide those directions. Topic sentences direct our anticipation and memory. By summarizing the main idea of the paragraph, they save us from the need to deduce the main idea from the material in a paragraph ourselves. Topic sentences also present us with one big idea to remember instead of several component ideas, thus helping us to keep track of the basic argument that is unfolding.

A topic sentence need not necessarily be the first sentence in a paragraph. For example, the first sentence might be a transition summing up preceding text and the second might announce the next topic. Or the topic sentence might be the last sentence, articulating what otherwise must be deduced from the content of the paragraph. And sometimes the "topic sentence" is not in fact a sentence, but a clause embedded in a longer sentence. Occasionally, but rarely, the subject of the paragraph is so obvious that a topic sentence is not necessary.

In addition to announcing topics, it is helpful to announce a change of topic or a change of perspective on that topic through the use of transition words or phrases. Each section, subsection, and often each paragraph of text should display some clear signal of its function, alerting the reader to the imminence of an example, addition, qualification, refutation, or other intellectual change of gear. Although transitions do pose the danger of falling into a ritual incantation of "further, moreover, finally" and "first, second, third," an uninspired "moreover" is still preferable to silence unless the unmarked transition is very obvious indeed.

A worse danger is the use of "crazy glue" transitions that do not usefully describe the relationship between sections or paragraphs, but simply stick them together. For example, although it has a proper use, "additionally" all too often signals that some miscellaneous ideas not inconsistent with the previous idea are being attached. "Conversely" has also gained entirely undeserved popularity among legal writers, who tend to use it as a signal that miscellaneous ideas different from the previous idea will follow. "As such" is another vague connector to avoid. If you are unclear in your own mind how paragraphs or larger chunks of text relate to each other, you have problems that cannot be solved with transition words or phrases—problems with small-scale organization or paragraph structure that your revision needs to address first.

The following passage, the conclusion of an article by Professor Cass Sunstein, makes effective use of topic sentences and transitions, which we highlight here in italics.

> *Analogical reasoning is the conventional method of the lawyer; it plays a large role in everyday thinking as well.* Its distinctive properties are a requirement of principled consistency, a focus on concrete particulars, incompletely theorized judgments, and the creation and testing of principles having a low or intermediate level of generality.
>
> *Because of its comparative lack of ambition, this form of reasoning has some important disadvantages.* Compared with the search for reflective equilibrium, it is insufficiently theoretical; it does not account for its own low-level principles in sufficient depth or detail. Compared with economics and empirical social science, it is at best primitive on the important issue of likely social consequences. Law should be more attuned to facts, and on this score analogical thinking may be an obstacle to progress.
>
> *But in a world with limited time and capacities, and with sharp disagreements on first principles, analogical reasoning has some beneficial features as well.* Most important, this form of reasoning does not require people to develop full theories to account for their convictions; it promotes moral evolution over time; it fits uniquely well with a system based on principles of stare decisis; and it allows people who diverge on abstract principles to converge on particular outcomes. In any case it is unsurprising that analogical reasoning continues to have enormous importance in legal and political discussion.
>
> *A notable aspect of analogical thinking is that people engaged in this type of reasoning are peculiarly alert to the inconsistent or abhorrent result, and they take strong convictions about particular cases to provide reasons for reevaluating their views about other cases or even about apparently guiding general principles.* The emphasis on particular cases and particular convictions need not be regarded as an embarrassment, or as a violation of the lawyer's commitment to principle. On the

> contrary, it should be seen as a central part of the exercise of practical reason in law (and elsewhere).
>
> *In this light, it seems most unfortunate that analogical reasoning has fallen into ill repute.* To abandon this method of reasoning may be to give up, far too quickly, on some of the most useful methods we have for evaluating our practices, and for deciding whether to change them through law.[8]

Here, the first sentence announces a topic ("analogical reasoning") and four major transitions ("because," "but," "a notable aspect," and "in this light") alert the reader that the writer's argument will proceed through an explanation, a qualification, an example, and a conclusion. With a clear itinerary thus in hand, the reader is ready and willing to follow.

E. POLISHING: PARAGRAPH STRUCTURE

When you have completed your revisions at the content and organization levels, the business of polishing paragraphs and sentences can begin. This is a satisfying stage of revision when meaning starts to shine through; try to leave ample time for it. Although they are dealt with separately here, the paragraph- and sentence-revision processes are of course inseparable in practice.

Effective paragraphs must exhibit *unity* and *cohesion*, that is, the ideas within each paragraph must not only bear on the idea expressed in the topic sentence (have unity), they must be meaningfully related to each other (show cohesion). Cohesion makes the difference between a satisfactory paper that a reader can struggle through with some profit and first-rate work that fully engages the reader's intellect and sympathies.

Even a unified paragraph with a clear topic sentence may nonetheless alienate your reader if it lacks cohesion. A list is not a paragraph, and strong transition words and phrases are helpful to the reader. Dovetailing is a technique to avoid choppy prose. Dovetailing puts new information at the end of sentences and old information at the beginning. Parallel sentence structure and the repeating of key words and phrases can be used to enhance cohesion.

As you have guessed by now, the previous paragraph fails because it lacks cohesion, although it has unity. Rewritten to take its own poorly expressed advice, it might read as follows.

Even a unified paragraph with a clear topic sentence
will alienate your reader if it lacks cohesion, that is, if it remains
a mere list of kindred ideas. One way to promote paragraph
cohesion is to use strong and accurate transition words or
phrases, remembering, however, that "and" is a very weak
transition. Another way to promote cohesion is to "dovetail"
your sentences, fitting them together as neatly as a carpenter
joins pieces of wood. In a series of dovetailed sentences, new
information appears at the end of sentences and old information
begins sentences. This technique does not entail the literal
repetition of information. Rather, it uses abstractions and
pronouns (like "technique" and "it") when new information
becomes old. Finally, in addition to dovetailing your sentences
and using strong transitions, you can promote cohesion by
repeating key words and phrases and by echoing the structure of
one sentence in another.

This rewritten paragraph makes use of explicit transitions.
"That is" implies that a definition follows, "one way" and "another
way" announce examples, "however" tells us that a further
qualification will follow, "rather" signals a correction, and "finally"
lets our overextended attention-span know that relief is just a sentence
or so away. In addition, the sentences on dovetailing are themselves
dovetailed, consistently hooking new information onto old.

As an exercise, read the two paragraphs that follow, the first
by Professor David Luban and the second by then law student Eric J.
Grannis. These two writers have composed paragraphs that have
unity and cohesion, texts that carry us along as we read them,
whether in the end we agree or disagree with the ideas expressed. As
you read, try to identify the techniques that make these strong
paragraphs.

<u>Example A</u>

Legal argument is a struggle for the privilege of
recounting the past. To the victor goes the right to infuse a
constitutional clause, or a statute, or a series of prior decisions
with the meaning that it will henceforth bear by recounting its
circumstances of origin and assigning its place in history. I shall
call such a historical placement of legal materials a *political
narrative*. A string of precedents, a legislative history, an
examination of framers' intent are all political narratives. To the
victor goes also the right to recite what I shall call the *local
narrative* constituting "the facts of the case at hand," and,
following on these two rights, the additional right to pronounce
the correspondence or mirroring of each narrative in the other
that renders further argument unnecessary.[9]

Example B

Some commentators have criticized Americans for becoming too thin-skinned, urging that painful controversy is one of the costs of a vigorous First Amendment. However, surely being so thick-skinned as to withstand rhetorical jabs does not entail being so thick-skulled as to withstand violent blows. For groups that have been traditional targets of bigotry, the toleration of their fellow citizens' speech advocating certain ideas will be a special burden, but that toleration is demanded by the Constitution. The Constitution does not demand, however, that such groups stoically bear the special burden of being selected for victimization on the basis of their race or other characteristics. Rather, the Constitution permits government to prevent the resulting disproportionate victimization and impediments to the exercise of liberties by imposing more severe penalties on bias-motivated crime. Thus, notwithstanding the decisions of two state supreme courts, statutes that enhance the penalties for bias-motivated crimes are valid under the First Amendment. Such statutes are facially content-neutral, and they advance many interests that are unrelated to the suppression of free expression without restricting First Amendment freedoms any more than is necessary to achieve those interests.[10]

Example A begins with a short, enigmatic topic sentence about the nature of legal argument that the rest of the paragraph artfully expounds. The repetition of the rather formal construction "to the victor goes..." structures the paragraph and creates an air of solemnity. Example B uses transitions to move the reader swiftly and logically along ("however...however...rather ...thus") to the writer's conclusion ("statutes that enhance the penalties for bias-motivated crimes are valid under the First Amendment"). Note that here the topic (the statutes are valid) is not stated at the beginning of the paragraph but is a general statement summarizing at the end what must otherwise be deduced. Note also the effective dovetailing of the first and second and third and fourth sentences.

F. POLISHING: SENTENCE-LEVEL REVISION

There are sentence-level problems that *must* be corrected, and those that *should* be corrected. Grammatical errors, missing or misplaced punctuation marks, and diction errors (wrong words) must be corrected. Such flaws distract all readers and offend many. They shake the reader's faith in your ideas. Thus, if you have problems with the mechanics of English, take the time to understand and banish from your writing the common grammatical mistakes detailed in Appendix A. Whether you have problems or not, your permanent library should include at least one grammar text. (Several are listed at the end of this chapter.) Similarly, if you cannot articulate the correct uses of the comma or the only two correct uses of the semicolon, you may need to spend time with Appendix B, on punctuation. (Do you believe that commas belong where you would pause if you were reading aloud? If so, you definitely need to read Appendix B. The "comma-when-you-pause" fallacy is responsible for many errors.)

Appendix A also discusses common usage and sentence structure problems—what you *probably should* as opposed to *absolutely must* fix. When we revise the structure of our sentences, we are almost always looking for greater clarity, for a more direct connection to the reader. But before we can cure our prose, we need a vocabulary for diagnosing its ills. Whether we are editing our own or someone else's writing, the epithets "wordy," "confusing," or "vague" are rarely helpful in themselves, no matter how accurate. But if we can see that vagueness can be caused by inappropriate use of the passive voice, wordiness by an overbearing compound subject, and confusion by a lack of parallelism, we are on our way to banishing unintended ambiguity. Appendix A aims to help you develop that vocabulary.

There is just one matter of usage discussed in Appendix A that is not, in our view, optional: avoiding sexist language. When one of our most prominent judges publicly exhorts lawyers to banish sexist language from their briefs, the subject is no longer controversial.[11] The minimal work of avoiding sexist language is more than compensated by the dignity it confers on our prose.

Finally, when your writing is correct and clear, there is one more step to go. Within the conventions of scholarly writing, you can develop your own style, find your own distinctive voice: it is authenticity that divides good from exceptional writing. Chapter Seven suggests ways to make your writing *more* than professional and effective.

G. POLISING: PROOFREADING

> *"Nobody is prefect."*
> *- The authors*

Proofreading someone else's work is a demanding job that calls on highly specialized skills; proofreading your own work is that and simple misery. The only thing worse, is discovering all those humiliating typographical errors after you have handed in your work. Moreover, even the friendliest reader is turned off by typographical errors and typographical inconsistencies (inconsistent spelling capitalization, or use of hyphens. Fairly or not, he effect of work that is carefully researched, thought out and written can be compromised if you do not allow enough time for an equally careful proofreading.

The first rule of proofreading is more in the nature of a warning: your computer's Spell-check program is just a beginning. Spell-checkers are a congenial time and embarrassment saver for all writers, and a positive blessing for people who simply can not cope with the eccentricities and infidelities of english spelling. But your spell-checker cannot detect wrong words or missing words. For instance, it will not fault you for typing "he" for "the" or "their for "there". In addition, spellcheckers do not speak the language of the law. For example, your computer will be undisturbed by "judgement" (a variant spelling aceptable in Standard American English) although in the American legal culture, "judgment" is the *only* correct spelling.

The second rule is harder to observe: read every word, do not skim. Reader anticipation is the enemy of proofreading: we see the words we expect to see. One of the most useful anti-browsing techniques simply to move a ruler or a sheet of blank paper under each line of text as you read, so that your eye can go no farther than the end of one line. Some writers force themselves to start at the end of their texts and read sentence-by-sentence toward the beginning. Whether you choose to endure this particular from of torture or not, it is a good idea to proofread the latter sections first, because they are more likely to have undetected errors. Be sure to proofread headings and epigrams as well as text. And check specifically to see that quotation marks, parentheses, and brackets all have their partners.

If you are writing for publication you *must* profread for typographical consistency as well as for accuracy; ;even if you are not writing for publication, you *should* read for consistancy. Foolish consistency may well be the hobgoblin of small minds, as Emerson said, but inconsistency certainly gives your paper an air of carelessness and unprofessionalism that puts off a serious reader and complicates a copy-editor's job. Be sure that all headings of equal weight are treated the same way. Be sure that your use of capitalization is consistent (If you are writing for Law Review, your capitalization must of course follow Bluebook style. And be sure that compound terms are consistently, as well as *correctly*, rendered: hyphenated, one word, or two words. When no prefered form can be found, choose one form and stick to it. For instance, WESTLAW and LEXIS can be described as "online" or on-line" services and one of their major uses as "fulltext" or "full-text" searches. We use "online" and "full-text," largely because the latter, a newer coinage, looks strange to us as one word. But in any event, you should make a list of recuring difficult words or terms so that you can refer to it as you proofread. (You can also use your computer to search and replace inconsistent usage.)

As you may have noticed, this section on proofreading is plaqued by common typos. Go back and proofread it carefully. Then look at the corrected version in appendix d. If you missed more than one, your proofreading skills need polishing.

REFERENCES FOR FURTHER READING

Style & Usage & Grammar

THEODORE BERNSTEIN, THE CAREFUL WRITER: A MODERN GUIDE
        TO ENGLISH USAGE, Atheneum (1984).
CLAIRE COOK, THE MLA'S LINE BY LINE: HOW TO EDIT YOUR
        WRITING, Houghton, Mifflin (1985).
FREDERICK CREWS, THE RANDOM HOUSE HANDBOOK (5th ed. 1988).
WILMA R. EBBITT & DAVID R. EBBITT, WRITER'S GUIDE & INDEX
        TO ENGLISH, Oxford University Press (8th ed. 1990).
WILSON FOLLET, MODERN AMERICAN USAGE: A GUIDE, Hill &
        Wang (1986).
DONALD HALL & SVEN BIRKERTS, WRITING WELL, Harper College
        (8th ed. 1993).
JOSEPH M. WILLIAMS, STYLE: TEN LESSONS IN CLARITY & GRACE,
        Harper Collins (4th ed. 1994); STYLE: TOWARD CLARITY &
        GRACE, University of Chicago Press (1990).

Manuscript Preparation

THE CHICAGO MANUAL OF STYLE, University of Chicago Press (14th
        ed. 1993).
TEXAS L. REV. ASSOCIATION, TEXAS LAW REVIEW MANUAL ON
        STYLE.
WORDS INTO TYPE, Prentice Hall, Inc. (3rd. ed. 1986).

NOTES

1.   For a more detailed discussion, see Lloyd F. Bitzer, *The Rhetorical Situation, in* PHILOSOPHY AND RHETORIC, Jan. 1968, at 1.

2.   489 U.S. 198 (1989)

3.   *See* Steve Finzio, Comment, *Prison Cells, Leg Restraints and "Custodial Interrogation": Miranda's Role in Crimes that Occur in Prison*, 59 U. CHI. L. REV. 719 (1992).

4.   David B. Oppenheimer, *Negligent Discrimination*, 141 U. PA. L. REV. 899 (1993).

5.   Finzio, *supra* note 3, at 721.

6.   Eileen M. Mullen, Note, *Rotating Japanese Managers in American Subsidiaries of Japanese Firms: A Challenge for American Employment Discrimination Law*, 45 STAN. L. REV. 725 (1993).

7.   Andrea Lewis, Note, *Drug Testing: Can Privacy Interests Be Protected Under the Special Needs Doctrine*, 56 BROOK. L. REV. 1013 (1990).

8.   Cass R. Sunstein, *On Analogical Reasoning*, 106 HARV. L. REV. 741, 790-91 (1993).

9.   David Luban, *Difference Made Legal: The Court and Dr. King*, 87 MICH. L. REV. 2152 (1989).

10.   Eric J. Grannis, *Fighting Words and Fighting Freestyle: The Constitutionality of Penalty Enhancement for Bias Crimes*, 93 COLUM. L. REV. 178, 230 (1993).

11.   Judith S. Kaye, *A Brief for Gender-Neutral Brief-Writing*, N.Y. L.J. Mar. 21, 1991.

CHAPTER SIX

FOOTNOTES[1] AND THE ETHICAL USE OF BORROWED MATERIALS

"Symbolically, of course, the footnote is of minor importance. It is relegated to the bottom of the page...[and] lives a life of exclusion and marginalization.... Yet simultaneously deconstruction argues that...the marginalization and exclusion necessary for intellectual conception is never complete. Traces of banished and deemphasized alternatives lurk within the dominant conception, supporting it and at the same time calling its dominance into question. This is the problem of the footnote writ large."

- J.M. Balkin

"Encountering [a footnote] is like going downstairs to answer the doorbell while making love."

- Noel Coward

---

[1] This chapter uses footnotes rather than endnotes. As a rule, textbook authors, unlike scholarly writers, use notes mainly to attribute borrowed materials to their sources. However, this chapter will also use authority footnotes and textual footnotes, in order to provide examples of scholarly practice. At the end of each footnote we will frequently explain the note's function(s) in brackets. [This is a textual footnote.]

87

Footnotes are a rich source of humor in legal academia, the lawyer's lawyer joke. Law review articles with as many as 1,000 footnotes and leviathan mazes of cross-references have prompted lengthy satires on footnote practice. For example, one writer has diagnosed the "Single-Sentence-String-Cite" Syndrome, the "Too-Many-Footnotes-To-Change-Text" Syndrome, and the "Musical Chair" cross-referencing Syndrome.[2] Another has exposed the practices of "footnote trashing"[3] and "footnote networking."[4] Yet, although this gleeful self-criticism accurately describes and rightly condemns some pretentious excesses, footnotes also serve important values—accuracy, honesty, and thoughtfulness—and there remains a lot of commonsense information about them that a novice needs to learn. This chapter discusses the theory and practice of footnoting and the related problems of plagiarism and fair use.[5]

As we noted in Chapter One, footnotes have three basic functions: (1) they provide authority for assertions, and in so doing, provide a bibliography for further research; (2) they attribute borrowed materials to their sources; and (3) they continue a discussion begun in the text, but along lines somewhat peripheral to

---

[2]   William R. Slomanson, *The Bottom Line: Footnote Logic in Law Review Writing*, 7 LEGAL REFERENCE SERVICES Q., 47, 56-58 (1987). [This footnote attributes borrowed material to its source.]

[3]   Arthur D. Austin, *Footnotes as Product Differentiation*, 40 VAND. L. REV. 1131, 1153 (1987). [This is an attribution footnote.]

[4]   "Publishing a stream of names in an author's note can sustain a movement to higher status and reputation. The tacit code assumes reciprocity: if you mention a colleague, he is obligated to use your name." *Id*. at 1146. [This footnote is textual in that it defines a term in the text. It also attributes the term to its author.]

[5]   Beyond the scope of this chapter are the format and typography of footnotes. This complicated matter is set out in THE BLUEBOOK, whose rules must be observed if you are writing a law review article for a journal that follows Bluebook style and should be observed in seminar papers. The footnotes in this chapter conform to Bluebook style. With its labyrinth of rules both commonsensical and arbitrary, THE BLUEBOOK itself is increasingly controversial. Some critics feel that sensible standards would serve as well as THE BLUEBOOK's rigid and tormenting prescriptions. Perhaps the best solution is that of the *Oklahoma City University Law Review*, which announces "text and footnotes in the *Review* conform to [the Bluebook], except where common sense dictates otherwise." 15 OKLA. CITY U. L. REV. unnumbered (Spring, 1990), cited in James W. Paulsen, *An Uninformed System of Citation*, 105 HARV. L. REV. 1780, 1785 n.40 (1992) (book review). [This textual footnote forestalls a potential criticism. It also contains citations that serve the authority, attribution, and bibliographic functions.]

the logical development of the primary argument. This chapter will discuss each of the three functions, but perhaps a few preliminary examples will make the distinctions clearer.

If we write, for example, that suspects in government custody must be informed of their constitutional rights before they may be questioned, we are stating a very general and settled legal proposition familiar to lawyers and laypersons alike. Yet the conventions of legal scholarship nonetheless require us to document this proposition with an *authority* footnote that cites *Miranda v. Arizona.*[6] If we further state that the lower federal courts have taken different approaches to *Miranda* in the prison context, we make a less obvious factual statement that also and more obviously requires documentation in an authority footnote. If, however, we adopt another writer's conclusion that the best solution to the problem of *Miranda* in prison is to require warnings only for inmates upon whom official suspicion has focused, we need to *attribute* that idea to its source, in this case the author of the article mentioned in Chapter Five.[7] Finally, if we wish to comment on that idea, but the comment is incidental or marginal to the subject under discussion, we might put our comments in a *textual* footnote.[8]

As you can see from these examples, authority and attribution are somewhat similar notions; sometimes one footnote serves both functions. But the need for authority footnotes is grounded in the conventions of the law and legal scholarship, while attribution is an ethical imperative—an absolute prohibition on the uncredited use of another writer's words or ideas.

A. AUTHORITY FOOTNOTES

As the examples above and the discussion in Part C of Chapter Five also suggest, legal scholarship is characterized by extensive documentation. Indeed, the genre's devotion to authority

---

[6]   384 U.S. 436 (1966).

[7]   Steve Finzio, Comment, *Prison Cells, Leg Restraints and 'Custodial Interrogation': Miranda's Role in Crimes that Occur in Prison*, 59 U. CHI. L. REV. 719 (1992).

[8]   We might, for instance, use a textual footnote to wonder whether the writer's proposed standard was so vague as to invite abuse from over-zealous prison authorities.

sometimes understandably appears (especially to writers) to be more like a mania. It may well be that legal scholarship has unthinkingly adopted the authority conventions of the judicial opinion, and that these rigid requirements need to be reconsidered by scholars. But whatever the origins and merits of authority footnotes, beginning scholars are well-advised to observe the ground rules, although well-known scholars may on occasion "take greater 'risks' in making statements for which there is presumably little or no authority."[9]

Professor Delgado tells the beginning scholar that authority footnotes must substantiate every proposition in the text, including every assertion of law or fact. The only exceptions, he says, are passages of pure argument, topic sentences, and conclusions.[10] Law review manuals often offer similar advice, requiring documentation of everything but the author's opinions, transitions, and conclusions.[11] In other words, the concept of "common knowledge," which exempts writers in some other disciplines from the duty to document information found in five or more sources, has almost no application to legal scholarship.

This is not to say that your every statement requires encyclopedic documentation. Background sections often need fewer and more general footnotes than analysis sections, particularly where the background information is not highly specialized. "See generally" and "see, e.g." cites can frequently be used in background footnotes.

But authority footnotes pose problems of degree as well as number for the writer, who has to decide not only how many footnotes to use, but also which, if any, "signal" to use in which footnotes. Signals principally let the reader know how strongly the authority in the footnote supports the proposition in the text. The Bluebook contains a clear and concise guide to their proper use.

---

[9]   Slomanson, *supra* note 2, at 55. [This is a footnote providing both authority for the proposition and attribution to the writer.]

[10]   Richard Delgado, *How to Write a Law Review Article*, 20 U.S.F. L. REV. 445, 451 (1986). [This is an authority footnote attributing borrowed material to its source.]

[11]   *See, e.g.*, Terri M. LeClercq, ed., *Plagiarism: Pilfered Paragraphs*, 8 THE SECOND DRAFT 1, (1993) (citing the MANUAL OF THE AMERICAN UNIVERSITY). [This authority footnote uses a signal cite to show there is support for the proposition made in the text.]

Legal scholarship not only requires the use of authority, it also forbids its misuse, whether in footnotes or text. Some writers distort their sources or use "no-signal" and "see" cites for sources that only partially support their viewpoints; others commit the even more heinous crime of fabricating data or authority. Needless to say, it is a breach of ethics to invent authority or use a source in a misleading manner. To avoid distorting sources, do not:

- quote a work out of context where to do so creates a misleading impression of its content, or
- paste together portions of a work in order to give it a meaning inconsistent with the work taken in its entirety.[12]

In addition, scholarship obliges writers to explain when cited authority does not squarely support the proposition in the text. For example, when you use "Cf." to suggest support by analogy, you are obliged to explain in a parenthetical. "See generally" creates a similar obligation.

Finally, authority footnotes—like *all* footnotes—should be sketched in as much detail as possible in your first draft. Although this creates renumbering and cross-referencing problems in later drafts, as you add or drop footnotes, footnoting early saves you the time and tedium of combing through your sources a second time.

B. ATTRIBUTION FOOTNOTES, PLAGIARISM, AND FAIR USE

An understanding of attribution footnotes begins with the recognition that credit is more than an academic courtesy. Like new law, which is constantly being fashioned out of existing rules, scholarly papers commonly build upon and advance ongoing intellectual debates. Thus reliance on the ideas of others is intrinsic to scholarly pursuits and is something to parade, not bury. Indeed, acknowledgment of our intellectual ancestors both establishes the quality of our research and provides useful references for readers who wish to delve into the subject matter.

---

[12] Michael L. Closen & Robert M. Jarvis, *The National Conference of Law Reviews Model Code of Ethics: Final Text and Comments*, 75 MARQ. L. REV. 509, 527 (1992). [Authority footnote.]

But acknowledgment is above all an ethical obligation, an obligation to give credit where credit is due. The failure to properly acknowledge the work of another, whether in footnote or text, lays a writer open to charges of academic dishonesty and plagiarism, the latter of which is commonly defined as the representation of the words or ideas of another as one's own. Moreover, and despite dissension on the issue, the legal and academic communities do not routinely regard an intent to deceive as a necessary element of plagiarism. Although lack of intent is often a mitigating factor in determining sanctions, many regard the negligent or reckless appropriation of another's work as plagiarism, even when it is the inadvertent product of careless research and note-taking.[13]

Proper acknowledgment of your sources requires you to conform to the following conventions:

1. Provide a footnote for borrowed language, facts or ideas whether quoted or paraphrased in your text.[14]
2. When you borrow seven consecutive words or more, use quotation marks; of course, where the wording is distinctive, it is appropriate to use quotation marks for fewer than seven words. (The text at footnotes 2-4 above provides examples of the latter situation.)
3. Put borrowed language in quotation marks when the quotation contains fewer than 50 words.
4. Use block quotes—that is indent and single-space quotations—when they are 50 words or more. When you indent and single-space quotations, do not use quotation marks.
5. In addition to providing an attribution footnote for paraphrases, introduce the borrowed material with some reference to its source. For example, "One recent commentator points out that...."

---

[13] *See generally*, Terri LeClercq, *Intent to Deceive*, 8 THE SECOND DRAFT 3 (1993). [This footnote provides authority for the proposition made in the text.]

[14] Although many composition texts will tell you that you do not need a footnote for "common knowledge," that is, for material found in five or more sources, as suggested above, such a rule of thumb is not applicable to legal scholarship. Although the fact of multiple sources might lessen the writer's ethical obligation somewhat, an *authority* footnote would still be necessary. [This is a textual footnote.]

6.   If you find a source through other sources, good research practice requires you to look up the cited source. Regardless of whether you do, however, citation convention requires you to footnote the citing source as well as the cited source if the citer's use of the cited source is original.

Finally, attribution footnotes should always be included in your very first draft: if you wait until the revision stage, paraphrased material may escape attribution altogether, causing inadvertent (but inexcusable) plagiarism.

The examples below should help you to distinguish between plagiarism and appropriately attributed use.

Original Material

The Crisis of Modern Jurisprudence:
Casey v. Planned Parenthood
Paul M. Zimmerman
20 Fictional L. Rev. 1, 13 (1993)

The most promising aspect of the joint opinion in *Casey v. Planned Parenthood*[1] was its sensitivity to critical race and critical feminist studies, specifically to their techniques of "looking to the bottom."[2] The *Casey* court listened to the stories of women who stood to suffer most when it struck down the spousal notification requirement of the Pennsylvania abortion regulation and affirmed that women have the right to abort pre-viability fetuses. Such a jurisprudential development may restore the court's institutional legitimacy by providing a normative basis for legal analysis.

---

1.   Casey, 112 S.Ct. 2791 (1992).
2.   Mari J. Matsuda, *Looking to the Bottom: Critical Legal Studies and Reparations*, 22 HARV. C.R. - C.L. L. REV. 323 (1987).

Overt Plagiarism

> The court's acceptance of legal storytelling techniques in *Casey v. Planned Parenthood*1 was an interesting development. The *Casey* court listened to the stories of women who stood to suffer most when it struck down the spousal notification requirement of the Pennsylvania abortion regulation and affirmed that women have the right to abort pre-viability fetuses. This approach may allow for the reconstruction of a coherent jurisprudence that restores the court's institutional legitimacy.
>
> ----------
>
> 1.   Casey, 112 S.Ct. 2791 (1992).

This example overtly plagiarizes the original article. The writer usurps the comment's thesis without acknowledgment. The first and third sentences of the passage are paraphrases that require a footnote attributing the content to the source. In addition, the writer retains the exact wording of the original in the second sentence but fails to surround the language with quotation marks.

Covert Plagiarism

> The *Casey* court's acceptance of legal storytelling techniques, its decision to "look to the bottom,"1 was an interesting development. "The *Casey* court listened to the stories of women who stood to suffer most when it struck down the spousal notification requirement of the Pennsylvania abortion regulation and affirmed that women have the right to abort pre-viability fetuses."2 This approach may allow for the reconstruction of a coherent jurisprudence that restores the court's institutional legitimacy.
>
> ----------
>
> 1.   Mari J. Matsuda, *Looking to the Bottom: Critical Legal Studies and Reparations*, 22 HARV. C.R-C.L. L. REV. 323 (1987).
> 2.   Paul M. Zimmerman, Note, *The Crisis of Modern Jurisprudence:* Casey v. Planned Parenthood, 20 FICT. L. REV. 1, 13 (1993).

This version covertly plagiarizes the original article. First, by citing to Professor Matsuda instead of to the casenote, the writer suggests she has read the cited source, although this may not be the case. Moreover, even if she had read Professor Matsuda, she must also cite the casenote because it was that author who had the idea to use Professor Matsuda in this context. Second, although the writer correctly places quotation marks around the language directly borrowed from the casenote, and also provides the appropriate footnote, the citation gives the erroneous impression that the quoted sentence is the only borrowed material in the paragraph. In fact, the ideas in the first and third sentences are also borrowed. To avoid a charge of plagiarism, the writer needs to acknowledge the author of the casenote at the outset ["As one commentator argues..."] and to add a footnote at the conclusion of her summary of the borrowed material, as in the example that follows.

Proper Attribution

As one commentator argues, the *Casey* court's acceptance of legal storytelling techniques, its decision to "look to the bottom," was an interesting development.[1] "The *Casey* court listened to the stories of women who stood to suffer most when it struck down the spousal notification requirement of the Pennsylvania abortion regulation and affirmed that women have the right to abort pre-viability fetuses."[2] This approach may allow for the reconstruction of a coherent jurisprudence that restores the Court's institutional legitimacy.[3]

---

1.   Paul M. Zimmerman, Note, *The Crisis of Modern Jurisprudence:* Casey v. Planned Parenthood, 20 FICT. L. REV. 1, 13 (1993), (quoting Mari J. Matsuda, *Looking to the Bottom: Critical Legal Studies and Reparations*, 22 HARV. C.R-C.L. L. REV. 323 (1987)).
2.   *Id.*
3.   *Id.*

Note that in this passage the author's attribution footnote correctly credits both the original and citing sources.

Finally, above and beyond proper attribution, writers and editors—especially those preparing a manuscript for publication—must be familiar with the concept of fair use in order to avoid copyright infringement. Fair use has to do with the extent to which you may use another's work, whether published or unpublished, without permission from the copyright holder. It balances copyright protection—which provides authors with an incentive for creating work that enriches society—against the public's need to use the work of others to promote knowledge and culture.[15] When courts determine whether the use of a work is fair, they consider four statutory factors:

1.   the purpose and character of the use, including whether such use is of commercial nature or is for nonprofit educational purposes;

2.   the nature of the copyrighted work;

3.   the amount and substantiality of the portion used in relation to the copyrighted work as a whole; and

4.   the effect of the use upon the potential market for or value of the copyrighted work.[16]

Because law reviews have an educational rather than commercial purpose, the first prong of the fair use doctrine does not present many obstacles to legal scholars. Since legal writers tend to borrow from copyrighted work of a scholarly nature, the second factor is also not especially problematic. With respect to the third factor, courts consider the proportion of quoted material in relation to the length of the source. You will almost certainly be safe if you stay within a 5% limit. Finally, note that the Court in *Harper & Row Publishers, Inc. v. The Nation Enterprises* stated that the fourth factor "is undoubtably the single most important element of fair use."[17]

---

[15]   KENNETH D. CREWS, COPYRIGHT, FAIR USE AND THE CHALLENGE FOR UNIVERSITIES: PROMOTING THE PROGRESS OF HIGHER EDUCATION 22-23 (1993). [Authority and attribution footnote.]

[16]   17 U.S.C. § 107 (1988). [This is an authority footnote.]

[17]   471 U.S. 539, 566 (1985). [Authority footnote.]

However, it is unlikely that scholarly use of copyrighted material will affect the source material's potential market or value. In general, therefore, fair use is given special deference when copyrighted material is used for a nonprofit educational purpose.[18] Nonetheless, when in doubt, seek permission.

C. TEXTUAL FOOTNOTES

Textual footnotes provide discursive commentary supplementing the text. They serve many purposes.

* Often they provide the reader with an example or illustration of a point made in the text, or they offer a needed definition.[19]

* Frequently they clarify or qualify an assertion made in the text.[20]

* Sometimes they raise a potential criticism or complication...and then proceed to address it or defer it to another day.[21]

* Increasingly, they are used for musing or for sharing with the reader an amusing anecdote or insight.

---

[18]   CREWS, *supra* note 16, at 23. [Authority and attribution footnote.]

[19]   Thus, for example, footnote 4 in this chapter defined a term used in the text. Note, by the way, that footnotes 19-22 in this chapter all serve an illustrative purpose.

[20]   For example, one writer added a qualifying footnote to the following sentence in the text: "The Supreme Court concluded that both *Smith* and *Jones* have defied consistent application by the lower courts." The footnote observed: "However, in support of the argument that *Smith* and *Jones* have defied consistent application, the Court could only muster the authority of a concurring opinion of one lower court judge."

[21]   *See, e.g., supra* note 5 and accompanying text. [Does it bother you to turn back? If so, curb your cross-references.]

Authors of this latter type of "personal" notes welcome the footnote as an opportunity to break with the objective, formal tone of legal writing.[22]

The phenomenon of the "personal" footnote crystallizes the larger debate over the value of textual footnotes. Many readers, especially practitioners and judges, find textual footnotes distracting—fit only for a reader with multiple personalities or split consciousness. The length and complexity of some textual footnotes make it difficult to resume reading the text without backtracking to pick up the threads of the argument. One prominent commentator remarked that "[i]f footnotes were a rational form of communication, Darwinian selection would have resulted in the eyes being set vertically rather than on an inefficient horizontal plane."[23] Thus, critics of textual footnotes prefer a "minimalist" style, in which footnotes are "devoid of interpretation or discursive commentary"[24] and exist only to provide authority and attribution. Others welcome the looser, exploratory nature of textual footnotes and regard them as but the first step toward a more conversational style in legal scholarship and an occasion for presenting embryonic ideas, alternate perspectives, and promising developments.[25]

As a writer, you will need to develop your own footnote style and discover whether you fall into the minimalist, centrist, or expansionist camp. But whether you use only a few textual footnotes

---

[22]   Indeed, adventurous authors like ourselves have been known to shift in footnotes from the conventional use of the third person to the first person. For an example of "personal" notes, see John Hart Ely, *Another Such Victory: Constitutional Theory and Practice in a World Where Courts Are No Different from Legislatures*, 77 VA. L. REV. 833 (1991).

[23]   Abner J. Mikva, *Goodbye to Footnotes*, 56 U. COLO. L. REV. 647, 648 (1985). [Attribution footnote.]

[24]   Austin, *supra* note 3, at 1143. [Attribution footnote.]

[25]   The quotation by J.M. Balkin that prefaces this chapter is representative of this position. Richard A. Matasar, Dean of Chicago-Kent College of Law, also regards diverse voices and discourse practices as an intellectual and ethical imperative: "The language of neutral principles, rationales, and holdings may be perceived as a cover for actual reasoning, the influence of culture, and the hold of ideology. Thus, today many legal scholars are searching for a new rhetoric that more candidly reveals the myriad ways that law is a reflection of very personal matters." *Storytelling and Legal Scholarship*, 68 CHI.-KENT L. REV. 353, 355 (1992). [Authority and textual footnote.]

or a great many, your decision whether to footnote or not to footnote should depend upon whether a textual footnote would be helpful to your reader. The point is not to prove you have thought of every conceivable tangential issue. The point is to provide textual footnotes that further enrich the paper's theme.

In making this determination, you will—as an editor of your own work or as a law review editor of another's work—occasionally find that you have put material into a footnote that is really central to the text, or, conversely, that you could tighten the text by relegating some peripheral matter in the text to a footnote.[26] Computers make it easy to move material between text and footnotes and thus aid us in deciding which position works best in each case.

---

[26] For instance, should we have put the discussion of THE BLUEBOOK in note 5 into the text instead?

CHAPTER SEVEN

WRITING WITH STYLE

"Most people don't realize that writing is a craft. You have to take your apprenticeship in it like anything else."

- Katherine Anne Porter

Scholarly writers traditionally privilege those stylistic conventions that suggest disinterested objectivity. They distance themselves from the text by writing exclusively in the third person. They efface themselves by using abstract language, instead of their own distinctive and ordinary vocabularies: "Given the second-best nature of the zero transactions cost equilibrium, it should not be surprising that the introduction of transactions has complex and ambiguous effects on contract choice, welfare, and optimal default choice." They depopulate the text with passive voice constructions: "This conclusion was reached no matter what legal theory was applied." And if forced to admit a personal interest in the debate, they scrupulously maintain the dual perspective of irony, understatement, or double negatives: "The analysis suggested here is not altogether disinterested." The upshot of such stylistic practices is that readers are often as much put off by the writer's prose as they are captivated by the writer's mind.

The worst of scholarly writing—prose that "sounds untouched by human hands, like a monstrous frozen dinner fabricated from sawdust and boiled crayons"[1]—can be avoided if you pursue a clean, clear style. To be readable, scholarly writers need only adhere to the prescriptive advice offered in Appendix A: avoid too many passives and nominalizations, make the grammatical subject the agent of the action, use forceful verbs, and keep the subject near the predicate and your modifiers near the modified. The prose that results will be concise and comprehensible and serviceable. It may also be faceless and flat. If you would like your prose to be not just competent, but to be special—to have a little panache and pizzazz—your task is harder. You will have to move beyond writing as communication toward writing as creative craft. You will have to develop your own style.

Good style is not mere idiosyncratic flourish; it is content. For example, we employ narrative style to root abstract discussions in a human context. We speak in the vernacular for straight talk. And when we change tone, vary diction, use metaphor, bend grammatical rules, we do so for a purpose. The stylistic technique underscores—even makes—our meaning. When it does not, when the technique is mere icing, we are better off sticking with the simple and efficient.

Good writing is above all honest writing that does not settle for cliches, jargon, hackneyed analogies, and worn-out metaphors. Rather, it is thoughtful and individual. Good writers are always present in their writing, however discreetly. The rest of this chapter focuses on some of the techniques writers use to leave an imprint on their texts.

A. MAKING THE MOST OF INTRODUCTIONS AND CONCLUSIONS

> *"Well begun is half done."*
> > *- Anonymous*

> *"All's well that ends well."*
> > *- William Shakespeare*

Given the relative brevity of introductions and conclusions, writers spend what might appear to be a disproportionate amount of time writing them. Such expenditure of energy is justified by their important functions and prominent positions. It is upon them, after all, that our readers form their first and final impressions of our work.

Introductions establish context. They delineate the perimeters of the forest while orienting the reader to some of the landmark trees; in other words, they identify the topic of the paper, locate the topic within the general literature on the subject, announce the thesis, and point toward the support offered and organization followed. If you manage to work all this essential information into the opening paragraphs, you have gone a long way toward fulfilling your readers' expectations, especially because readers of scholarly articles tend to have a prior interest in the topic and thus require little more motivation than clear exposition to peruse the piece. Nonetheless, some readers might need an additional incentive, and most readers appreciate a fresh presentation of the material. Thus a captivating, provocative opening is always worth a little extra trouble.

Similarly, the best conclusions end with a bang, not a whimper. As your last word on the topic, conclusions tend to be remembered, and thus deserve special crafting. While a conclusion is not the place to raise new issues, the best reach beyond brief restatement of your thesis and major arguments. Mere summary is anti-climactic. Instead, suggest avenues for additional investigation or emphasize the important implications of your analysis. Most of all, leave the reader excited about the subject matter and interested in exploring it further.

To put a little punch in your introduction or conclusion, you might want to try using narrative. Alternatively, you might want to open with a quote or with a forceful, provocative statement.

1. Use Narrative

Increasingly, part of the context that must be established in an introduction is the human and social context out of which legal issues emerge. Often that context is best realized through narrative.

James Boyd White tells us that because all legal issues begin and end "in ordinary language and experience, the heart of the law is the process of translation by which it must work, from ordinary language to legal language and back again."[2] In thinking about this statement, we realized that some of the most engrossing casenotes and comments that we have read follow this pattern. The article opens with a narrative in ordinary language, sometimes even a first-person narrative, about a legal problem. The body of the article then translates the narrative into legal language and analyzes the legal issues. Finally, the conclusion returns us to the ordinary world and reminds us of the impact of the law on human lives.

Personal narrative quickly engages the reader's interest in the following introduction to a student law review article on plagiarism and copyright infringement.

> A few years ago, while working as an editor, I was putting the finishing touches on a forthcoming book about an event from fifty years before, which had previously been chronicled by participants, observers, and scholars. The new book was nothing to get excited about, but it was well organized and comprehensive; it offered a new interpretation of the event; and its author, who had written several books before, had apparently done a competent job.

> One day the mass-transportation system broke down and I was unable to reach my office. Instead I went to my local library to verify some historical information for the book. As I browsed through one of the other books on the same subject in the library's collection, scanning the pages for names and dates, a passage caught my eye—a passage that was strangely, even disturbingly, familiar. The same passage appeared almost word for word in the manuscript I had been editing. With increasing agitation I paged through the remaining books. In the end, I identified five passages that my author appeared to have lifted from three different sources.[3]

Not all effective narrative is personal. Storytelling enlivens the introduction to an article finding a right in state constitutions for community treatment of the mentally ill.

> On January 17, 1993, Christopher Battiste, a homeless man from New York, was arrested for bludgeoning eighty-year-old Doll Mamie Johnson to death in front of her church in the Bronx. Mentally ill for much of his life, Battiste had spent years "drift[ing] in and out of jails, homeless shelters and psychiatric emergency rooms." Less than two months later, Larry Hogue, notorious for his very public and very bizarre behavior on the Upper West Side, was ordered by a state appeals court to be civilly committed for six months in a psychiatric center in Queens. At the same time that these events were transpiring in New York, similar stories were being told in cities across the United States.[4]

Many conclusions also make impressive use of narrative, returning the reader—after whole sections of abstract analysis—to the impact the analysis might have in human terms. Personal narrative is effectively used in the conclusion of the following casenote to ground its criticism of a decision upholding a state's right to display the Confederate flag.

> It is the spring of 1984 in Atlanta, and the groundskeeper at Franklin Delano Roosevelt High School is starting his morning routine In my twelfth grade homeroom we have finished the morning business—attendance has been taken, the announcements have been made. We are simply waiting for the bell to signal the start of the first class period. As I wait, my eyes return to the groundskeeper, who is carefully unfurling and raising a series of flags. First is the American flag, last is the Atlanta Public Schools flag, and sandwiched between the two is the Georgia State flag. I am drawn to this flag, particularly to its wholesale incorporation of Dixie. ...
>
> ... My eyes close tightly, my fists clench, and I slowly force from my mind images of the flag, of the Ku Klux Klan, of Bull Connor and George Wallace—of black people in chains, hanging from trees, kept illiterate, denied the opportunity to vote.
>
> The bell has rung. My teacher is calling my name: "James, are you ok?" I look up, startled. "Yes ma'am, I'm fine," I say, as I collect my books and head for class. ... But overcoming the flag has taken a piece of me—a piece that I will not easily recover.[5]

2. *Open or Close with a Quotation*

A striking quotation is a stylish way to begin—whether you use it as an epigram or in your opening sentences. Either way, the quotation is meant to spark the reader's interest by being either reflective and learned, or impertinent, humorous, and provocative (as in the example that follows).

> "Poetry is indispensable," Jean Cocteau once said, "if only I knew what for." Nearly everyone seems to agree that blackmail is an indispensable part of a well-developed criminal code, but no one is sure what for.[6]

Similarly, one effective way to close a piece is with a provocative, wise, or humorous quotation. Your own extended analysis can often be strikingly reinforced by an apt comment made by another author.

> Perhaps this pluralistic emphasis reflects the bias of someone who is struggling to finish the second edition of a treatise that tries to embrace the clash of competing constitutional visions. But I think my emphasis reflects something deeper than that. For me, the Constitution's greatness is in large measure its resistance to ideological reductionism—its resistance to neat encapsulation in any one grand tradition that defines the

aspirations of some of the dispossessed as outside the boundaries of the constitutive and defining charter of the society.

Is the Constitution, then, sometimes at war with its own premises? Perhaps it speaks in the words of Walt Whitman: "Do I contradict myself? Very well then, I contradict myself. I am large, I contain multitudes."[7]

3. *Begin Quickly and End Forcefully*

Many solid papers begin informatively. They open with statements about the significance of a subject, they provide essential summaries of background information, or they review relevant literature in order to highlight the contribution of the present work. Such introductions are competent—but slow.

It is a refreshing change to read a piece that begins quickly and forcefully. Good openings have a little drama. They may start with a "punchy" controversial statement, as in the following statement, which appeared in a symposium volume honoring the very decision the author seemingly deflates.

> *Goldberg v. Kelly* does not rank with the most important decisions in the history of the Supreme Court. It did not establish judicial review, as did *Marbury v. Madison*. Nor did it usher in the Civil War, as did *Scott v. Sandford*. It did not legitimate Jim Crow in the South, as did *Plessy v. Ferguson*, nor did it help undo it as did *Brown v. Board of Education*. It did not stand testimony to substantive due process or economic liberties, as did *Lochner v. New York*, nor did it create a constitutional right to abortion as did *Roe v. Wade*. *Goldberg v. Kelly* did not launch a war or define a generation. Although thundering greatness shall forever elude it, *Goldberg* nonetheless rates at the top of the second tier of great Supreme Court cases....[8]

A good introduction may also challenge established critical positions and fundamental assumptions.

> Wifely submission is risky business in the 1990s. Gone is the day when a wife could depend on her husband's labor to maintain her at home, "secure and safe." Today is the day of divorce at will and equality rhetoric, which means that if her marriage ends, the homemaker wife will be catapulted into financial independence, and probably ruin. Such is the 1990s price tag for choosing to "play with dolls."[9]

Good introductions may be a bit unconventional—as in the following opening, which trades on surprise, if not shock.

> What is pornography or obscenity? Except for those who profit by selling pictures of vaginas, the Supreme Court's various definitions of obscenity have been unsuccessful, at least in practice.[10]

Humor can also be good bait to hook your reader.

> (1)
> Banking law appears to be the preferred habitat for a peculiar genre of legal doctrine, the oxymoron. We have the nonbank bank, the nonthrift thrift, the nonbranch branch, even, as of 1992, the nonstatute statute. In this paper, we examine another oxymoron in banking law, the nondeposit deposit, by which we mean an instrument or account that fulfills the functional purposes of a checking account deposit but is not treated as a deposit for purposes of federal deposit insurance, Federal Reserve Board requirements, or both.[11]
> (2)
> Defying good advice, I entitled this lecture "Surviving Victim Talk." I wanted to call it "Beyond Victim Talk," but one friend told me she never reads anything that begins with "beyond." Another said he once attended a lecture entitled "Beyond Nihilism" and thought nothing of it. Still another friend reports that titles that begin with "beyond" or "towards" are like restaurants that say "all you can eat" or "a meal in itself"—all to be read as warnings to stay away.[12]

Conclusions also gain strength when they offer a fresh perspective on the familiar.

> Most individuals enter into employment contracts with hopes and dreams. Few enter with the end of the relationship clearly in mind. Still fewer anticipate that their employer will be able to prevent them from working elsewhere should they wish to leave. Would employees willingly enter employment relationships that so compromised their satisfaction, their personal autonomy, and maybe even their dignity if the situation unexpectedly deteriorated? Or would they enter these relationships only if they had no real choice, if they were impelled by necessity to work, and if they were unable to influence the terms? Perhaps, they would remain, despite unsatisfactory working conditions, only for the income or for love of the work, if the alternative was not to be able to do the work at all.. But that is a far cry from the American ideal of free labor.[13]

Another effective closing is to use the conclusion to encourage the reader to explore other promising avenues of discussion.

But as we reread and rewrite, we wonder whether we are proposing too much too late: too much because integrating even half of the close-reading practice we describe would radically transform the traditional two-credit advanced writing syllabus. (Might it find a place in a three-credit advanced writing course or a whole new course in Reading and Writing the Law?) And do our suggestions come too late in that we have accepted too readily an unexamined, perhaps ungrounded, assumption that critical reading can effectively be taught only after the first-year student's initiation into the discourse community? (Should the teaching of close reading be integrated into Legal Writing? Into Legal Process?) As we continue to teach and to read, the need for ever earlier training in critical thinking seems ever more apparent and urgent.[14]

Finally, conclusions are memorable when they go out with some straight talk, rendered perhaps with a light touch.

The Bluebook began as a simple concept: a short citation guide for those contributing articles to law reviews. It has grown, however, like poison ivy. *The Bluebook* now acts as a general citation manual, a style book, a brief-writer's guide, and a bibliographic resource for American, foreign, and international law materials. This is too much to expect of any temporary committee of students, no matter how gifted they may be.... In the next edition, instead of looking for new worlds of citation to conquer, perhaps *The Bluebook*'s editors should just try again, but this time get it right. To paraphrase Harvard Law's own Professor Kingsfield (or was it John Houseman): *The Bluebook* should get respect the old-fashioned way—by earning it.[15]

B. CREATIVE SYNTAX

1. *The Syntax of Conversation*

There is a trend among nonfiction writers to use ordinary language, to recreate for the reader the writer's train of thinking, to speak as persons with acknowledged interest in the subject matter. Moreover, this trend is not the province of journalists or "docu-dramatists" alone; it is happening in academic circles. If you are writing an informal essay or commentary, if you are incorporating narrative into your text, or if you simply want to imbue your prose with some of the vibrancy of natural speech, you might decide to adopt a conversational style.

A conversational style requires you to write sentences that have the structure of spontaneous thought, that is, your sentences must produce the illusion of mind in action—its flashes of insight, shifts of direction and tone, subjective interjections. Paradoxically, a lot of revision is often required to produce a pointed, "natural" sentence; early attempts may simply sound vacuous. Here are some tips to help you get started.

a.   To suggest a mind unpacking and refining an idea, use apposite rephrasings or cumulative modifiers that hone and extend the generalization of the main clause.

> (1)
> Time and again, right-of-publicity plaintiffs are described by the courts as carefully "cultivating" their talents, slowly "building" their images, judiciously and patiently "nurturing" their publicity values—as working long and hard to make themselves famous, popular, respected, beloved.[16]
> (2)
> The Constitution is many things, but it is first a written text, words arranged for all to read.[17]

b.   To incorporate personal commentary on abstract ideas, tack it on to the end of a sentence or interject it into the middle.

> (1)
> Simply put, are secret searches and seizures reasonable? Regardless of one's answer, at least one will be asking the right question—talking sense rather than nonsense.[18]
> (2)
> The need for communal approbation—the ultimate vulnerability in writing—is, if anything, greater for judges than for other writers.[19]

Notice how often punctuation marks are used to herald an author's personal commentary, rather than the more obvious use of the first person singular. Subjective remarks are surrounded by parentheses, set off with dashes, or preceded by commas or ellipses. Similar signals often alert readers to humorous or ironic remarks.

> (1)
> Or, if prejudice is a word that signified only what existed "back" in the past, don't we need a new word to signify what is going on in the present? Amnesia, perhaps?[20]
> (2)
> Victims can get on the agenda, the evening news, and the gossip circuit—victims get time.[21]

c.　To record questions, sudden insight, strong emotion, or shifts of thought, create a sense of movement by using rhetorical questions, parentheticals, and, even, snippets of sentences.

(1)

The Fourth Amendment today is an embarrassment. Much of what the Supreme Court has said in the last half century—that the Amendment generally calls for warrants and probable cause for all searches and seizures, and exclusion of illegally obtained evidence—is initially plausible but ultimately misguided. As a matter of text, history, and plain old common sense, these three pillars of modern Fourth Amendment case law are hard to support; in fact, today's Supreme Court does not really support them. Except when it does. Warrants are not required—unless they are. All searches and seizures must be grounded in probable cause—but not on Tuesdays. And unlawfully seized evidence must be excluded whenever five votes say so. Meanwhile, sensible rules that the Amendment clearly does lay down or presuppose—that all searches and seizures must be reasonable, that warrants (and only warrants) always require probable cause, and that the officialdom should be liable for unreasonable searches and seizures—are ignored by the Justices. Sometimes.[22]

(2)

The canonical blackmail problem is quickly stated. Busybody says to Philanderer: "Pay me $10,000, or I'll reveal your affairs to your wife." Busybody is guilty of blackmail. What is strange, however, is that if Busybody had actually revealed Philanderer's affairs, or if he had threatened Philanderer with doing so but not mentioned the money, or if he had asked for the money but not mentioned what he was going to do if he didn't get it—if he had done any one of these things, he would not be guilty of any crime whatsoever. Yet when he combines these various innocent actions, a crime results—blackmail. How odd; how mysterious; how come?[23]

d.　To acknowledge a personal interest in the subject matter and to engage your reader, use the first person.

I represent "bad mothers" because I need the truths they tell me concerning our common culture. They tell truths by exposing to me our likeness and our differences. I see myself reflected in them sometimes, recognizing in their gestures and their attitudes variations of ones familiar to me because they are my own. Beyond that though, in their *difference* they tell me truths. They tell me truths when they refuse to let me see who they are, when they hold a mirror facing me, between themselves and me, so that I confront that mirror as a barrier.[24]

2. *The Syntax of Ceremony*

Although writers often begin conversationally—with a "hook," a narrative, anecdote, or joke, that draws attention—there are occasions and topics which seem to call for a deeper note. On these occasions, you may want to raise your prose to a fitting level of resonance and formality. Writers often achieve ceremonial elegance by writing lengthy sentences with tightly coordinated, parallel structures.[25] Here are some tips.

a.   To give your sentences rhythm, balance phrase against phrase, clause against clause in symmetrical patterns. Such symmetry is useful in highlighting similarity and dissimilarity because the parallel sequences invite clear-cut comparisons.

> To assert that the judicial choice between honoring the dictates of conscience and affirming civic unity is an easy one is a sure sign of an impoverished imagination. To proclaim that in America today such questions of constitutional meaning are amenable to the formal methods of conventional legal argument is to misunderstand both the limits of legality and the nature of moral choice. And to confuse advocacy with scholarship only ensures that one will, in the end, fail at both.[26]

Symmetry can also be achieved if you balance the subject against the object.

> (1)
> [S]urely being so thick skinned as to withstand rhetorical jabs does not entail being so thick skulled as to withstand violent blows.[27]
> (2)
> [T]hose who deploy power in the struggle to achieve justice must...sometimes employ bad soldiers in the service of a good cause.[28]

b.   Another way to achieve eloquence is to end sentences with a series of cumulative, parallel statements. When you are lengthening a sentence by attaching coordinate statements to the end, cadence improves if each element is longer than the one before it.

> In California, the death penalty is not just a ferociously contested moral issue but a political metaphor: for some, the penalty is a sign of the repressiveness of the state, of the cruelty of all constituted authority, perhaps even of man's overreaching, a kind of ultimate anti-ecological hubris; for others, opposition to the penalty is the emblem of the lax, indulgent, sentimental distaste for all authority, of the disposition to lavish concern on those

who break society's rules at the expense of those who keep them, or a pseudoprofessionalism that finds excuses for every delict and deviation—in sum a last vestige of the dreadful sixties.[29]

c.   Sophistication is the mark of sentences that conclude with a summative, resumptive, or free modifier that follows your main clause.[30]

A resumptive modifier repeats a key noun, verb, or adjective from the main clause and then goes on to elaborate on it.

> Finally, women should educate themselves about the typically simple *procedures* for filing complaints against taxi drivers who make harassing comments to passengers—*procedures* that may result in suspension or deprivation of the cabdriver's license.[31]

A summative modifier sums up in a noun or phrase the main idea in the sentence and then elaborates.

> (1)
> [T]he outcomes of the six cases were driven by a deep recognition of law's indeterminate nature and of the inherently creative role of judge and juror—*a vision* that cannot tolerate excluding people with divergent perspectives from the creative act of adjudication.[32]
> (2)
> Basically, *The Bluebook* suffers from a bad case of federal parochialism—a pervasive *belief* that state courts simply are not important.[33]

Free modifiers follow the verb but comment on the grammatical subject of the sentence.

> *The law* is itself a product of the human creative process—*shaped* by centuries of tradition, renewed by the infusion of the new and the rediscovery of the old, continually rethought, reanalyzed, and reconstructed, as powerful and moving as any other work of literature.[34]

d.   Correlative conjunctions can be effectively used for emphasis and balance. Correlative conjunctions are conjunctions used in pairs.

> not only...but also...
> either...or...
> neither..nor...
> both...and...
> whether... or....

Because they are used to emphasize that two items are involved, the two items connected with correlative conjunctions should be parallel in construction to emphasize the comparison, as in the sentence that follows.

> The creative process is one of change, *both* for the creators, who while transforming their raw materials into new, finished works find themselves transformed, *and* for their audiences, who in seeking knowledge and enlightenment assimilate and transform those works as part of their own creative process.[35]

e.   Finally, eloquence improves when sentence length is varied and used to underscore the message. Short parallel sentences convey urgency, emphasis, and strong emotion.

> This is a true story. It is the story of how the law punished a man for speaking about his legal rights; of how, after punishing him, it silenced him; of how, when he did speak, he was not heard. This pervasive and awful oppression was subtle and, in a real way, largely unintentional. I know because I was one of his oppressors. I was his lawyer.[36]

Long sentences frequently achieve a cadence that suggests a sense of weightiness, high resolve, responsibility, and thoughtful exploration.

> (1)
>
> When conventional language is inadequate, when the hope of achieving justice through law collapses, when despair is deepest, the lyric of the street and the shop floor may best reflect what it is like to work for a living in an era that has contempt for work, workers and their lives.[37]
>
> (2)
>
> There is a glory, it seems, in the mystery of a language that can be deciphered only by initiates of the secret society; there is a great sense of power and an even greater actuality of power in controlling a language that in turn controls the most pressing affairs of individuals and communities; and there is a monopolistic safety in being able to manipulate a language which because it was part of the creation of legal problems must be part of their solutions as well.[38]

C. DICTION

> *"Cliches are little cinder blocks of crushed and reprocessed experience."*
>
> *- Donald Hall*

One of the central ways we are present in our writing is in our "diction" or choice of words and in our use of figures of speech. It is primarily with words that we establish tone—be it conversational or formal. It is with words that we convey our attitude toward the reader and the subject matter. And it is in our choice of words that we either hit the nail on the head or—as in the following example— miss the mark.

> Much of the innovation in capital market contracts can be *decomposed* into three continuing developments.

One of the most important qualities of a writer is sensitivity to words—to their denotations (explicit meanings) and connotations (implicit meanings or associations). Connotation plays a central role in the following sentence.

> Seriously at risk are the heroines of the Betty Crocker culture, women who have already devoted their most career-productive years to homemaking and who, if forced into the labor market after divorce, suddenly will be viewed as modern dinosaurs.[39]

With a stroke, "Betty Crocker" conjures up women of the 1950s, an entire generation of mothers baking in kitchens that are kept clean with labor-savings appliances. And, with another stroke, such women are relegated to a past as distant as the dinosaurs.

If a picture is worth a thousand words, so the right figure of speech or metaphor will save you a hundred.

> Fourth amendment case law is like a sinking ocean liner—rudderless and badly off course—yet most scholarship contents itself with rearranging the deck chairs.[40]

It is because language can be so evocative and precise that Donald Hall, a poet and teacher, tells us quite rightly that there are no synonyms in English. "Some words," he says, "are close to each other in meaning, close enough to reveal that they are not the same."[41] Although "to emulate" and "to ape" may be listed as synonyms, he illustrates, emulation implies imitation for the purpose of self-improvement while "aping" suggests imitation for the purpose of mockery. A thesaurus, he warns, is useful mostly for reminding us of the denotative and connotative differences between words that resemble each other.[42] Thus, careful writers spend time finding the words that express rather than approximate their meanings. They search for words that accord with their style and message.

In the scholarly context, problems arise when a writer uses academic discourse deceitfully—or simply unthinkingly. An author who writes "The child care provision is needs-based and, arguably, will involve a grievous loss if improperly denied" is not considering the effect his prose will have on his reader. The habit of hiding one's feelings under the garb of academic discourse is so ingrained that the author may not even realize that some might find his good intentions blurred by the seeming callousness of "arguably will involve grievous loss."

One way to avoid insensitivity to language is to restate in the vernacular a point made in formal language: a grass roots explanation or illustration is often a healthy reminder of an argument's practical significance and a refreshing check on pomposity.

> (1)
> Plagiarism dwells at the meeting place of two great human endeavors: literature and the law. It is the source of legal and critical disputes, an example of *"creativity gone bad."*[43]
> (2)
> If most government decisionmaking were decentralized today, cities would selfishly seek to evade responsibility for problems ranging from the disposal of toxic waste to the location of centers for the homeless ("*Not In My Backyard*").[44]

Beware also of confusing formal language, which is often appropriate, with language that is merely "fancy." Simple words are often dignified words, while fancy words are empty and pretentious. For example, "rich," "tool," and "ease," are simple yet formal, but "wealthy," "implement," and "facilitate" are fancy.[45] The elegance of ordinary language is demonstrated in the following passages.

> (1)
> Nothing is of more immediate practical importance to a lawyer than the rules that govern his own strategies and maneuvers; and nothing is more productive of deep and philosophical puzzles than the question of what those rules should be.[46]
> (2)
> [M]ost cases that reach the Supreme Court, at least, are hard—decent and intelligent people could vote either way and in fact have usually done so—and in an important sense what most

distinguishes the work of a good judge is not the vote but the achievement of mind....[47]

As for the deceitful use of language, it worth observing that even naive readers pick up false notes. Mock humility, insincere flattery, sarcasm, or fake candor are more likely to damage the author than the audience.

D. MIXING STYLES

Some of the best writing combines the conversational and the formal, yoking formal language with casual syntax, or weaving street talk into sophisticated syntactical structures.

(1)

> At its most extreme, realism views a court not as a syllogism machine, but as a sausage factory, where it doesn't much matter what goes into the product as long as it tastes good. Under a sausage factory view of adjudication, a judge is not a skilled mechanic, but a short order cook. The value of her work is measured, not by the rigor of the search for proper ingredients, but by the extent to which the final product conforms to the tastes of the best customers.[48]

(2)

> It is precisely to resolve the most difficult, the most uncertain, disputes that we have judges. Compelled to decide such cases, many judges pretend—sometimes to themselves as well as to the world—that what they have done is added two and two and gotten four, so that anyone who disagrees with their decision is crazy, or that what they have done is chosen Right over Wrong, so that anyone who disagrees with the decision is morally obtuse.[49]

The varied texture of this kind of writing keeps the reader alert and interested. Carefully calculated shifts from the elegant to the vernacular and vice-versa can summon laughter, righteous indignation —or, as in the example below, eulogy.

> At least in the years I knew him, Thurgood Marshall wasn't hot on celebrations. He had a vast capacity for joy and for sharing joy, and a fierce pride in the advances that civil rights had made in his lifetime. But he was too intensely aware of the work yet undone to waste his time reflecting on the past except as prologue.[50]

A mixed style conveys passionate feelings about another subject in the following passage.

> If lawyers have, by their words, alienated the individual nonlawyer; if the threat of litigation now must coerce the straightforward discourse that Jefferson always used when addressing a lay audience; if potential clients now think twice before retaining a clumsy wordsmith to verbalize the sensitive moments in their lives—yet the profession faces even a greater risk regarding the outside world. The lawyer's place as the arbiter and the rhetorician of the nation's values may have been permanently surrendered. No longer does a James Madison or Daniel Webster or an Abraham Lincoln fashion the Republic's aspirations by linking them to simple but elegant speech.
>
> No. For, as a result of a pitched battle across a decade and before television audiences of millions, the verbal struggle has been lost. And who now dominates the discursive center? Not the creative writers; their voices are dispersed and idiosyncratic. Surely not the preachers; they are in disarray or in jail. Not even the journalists, who have sacrificed whatever prose power they once had to the twenty-second sound bite and the pretty face. The winners and at least temporary rhetorical champions are ... the military.[51]

E. Some Final Thoughts

Like all things worth cultivating, a good prose style takes time and hard work. There is no guaranteed program, but three habits are almost certain to help. First, read as much good writing as you can. We instinctively imitate what we read—this is why first efforts at persuasive writing often sound like a judicial opinion—and if we read only sloppy, empty, and pretentious prose, that is what we will write. Second, write a lot, at the end of every school day if you can. By articulating in prose what you think you learned from the day's classes or clinics, how you feel about it, and what confuses you, you reinforce what you have learned, clarify your questions, and keep your writing and thinking muscles toned. Finally, when you edit and polish your own work, be a pitiless critic capable of throwing out whole pages that do not measure up. As writing teacher Peter Elbow points out, to be a good writer you have to be a big spender.[52]

NOTES

1. DONALD HALL, WRITING WELL 126 (1973).

2. James B. White, *Rhetoric and Law: the Arts of Cultural and Communal Life,"* in THE RHETORIC OF THE HUMAN SCIENCES: LANGUAGE AND ARGUMENT IN SCHOLARSHIP AND PUBLIC AFFAIRS 305 (John S. Nelson et al. eds., 1987).

3. Laurie Stearns, Comment, *Copy Wrong: Plagiarism, Process, Property, and the Law*, 80 CAL. L. REV. 513, 514 (1992).

4. Antony B. Klapper, *Finding a Right in State Constitutions for Community Treatment of the Mentally Ill*, 142 U. PA. L. REV. 739,741 (1993).

5. James Forman, Jr., Note, *Driving Dixie Down: Removing the Confederate Flag from Southern State Capitols*, 101 YALE L.J. 505, 526 (1991).

6. Leo Katz, *Blackmail and Other Forms of Arm-Twisting*, 141 U. PA. L. REV. 1567 (1993).

7. Laurence H. Tribe, *The Idea of the Constitution: A Metaphor-morphosis*, 37 J. LEGAL EDUC. 170, 173 (1987).

8. Richard A. Epstein, *No New Property*, 56 BROOK. L. REV. 747 (1990).

9. Cynthia Starnes, *Divorce and the Displaced Homemaker: A Discourse on Playing with Dolls, Partnership Buyouts and Dissociation Under No-Fault*, 60 U. CHI. L. REV. 67, 69-70 (1993).

10. James Lindgren, *Defining Pornography*, 141 U. PA. L. REV. 1153, 1155 (1993).

11. Jonathan R. Macey & Geoffrey P. Miller, *Nondeposit Deposits and the Future of Bank Regulation*, 91 MICH. L. REV. 237 (1992).

12. Martha Minow, *Surviving Victim Talk*, 40 UCLA L. REV. 1411, 1412 (1993).

13. Lea S. VanderVelde, *The Gendered Origins of the* Lumley *Doctrine: Binding Men's Consciences and Women's Fidelity*, 101 YALE L.J. 775, 852 (1992).

14. Elizabeth Fajans & Mary R. Falk, *Against the Tyranny of Paraphrase: Talking Back to Texts*, 78 CORNELL L. REV. 163, 204-05 (1993).

15. James W. Paulsen, *An Uninformed System of Citation*, 105 HARV. L. REV. 1780, 1794 (1992) (book review).

16. Michael Madow, *Private Ownership of Public Image: Popular Culture and Publicity Rights*, 81 COLUM. L. REV. 125, 182 (1993).

17. Robert A. Ferguson, *"We Do Ordain and Establish": The Constitution as Literary Text*, 29 WM & MARY L. REV. 3 (1987).

18.   Akhil R. Amar, *Fourth Amendment First Principles*, 107 HARV. L. REV. 757, 803 (1994).

19.   Robert A. Ferguson, *The Judicial Opinion as Literary Genre*, 2 YALE J. L. & HUMAN. 201, 217 (1990).

20.   PATRICIA J. WILLIAMS, THE ALCHEMY OF RACE AND RIGHTS 103 (1991).

21.   Minow, *supra* note 12, at 1414-15.

22.   Amar, *supra* note 18, at 758-58.

23.   Katz, *supra* note 6, at 1567.

24.   Naomi R. Cahn, *Inconsistent Stories*, 81 GEO. L.J. 2533, 2566 (1993).

25.   For a sophisticated discussion, see JOSEPH M. WILLIAMS, STYLE: TOWARD CLARITY AND GRACE, ch. 8 (1990).

26.   Paul F. Campos, *Advocacy and Scholarship*, 81 CA. L. REV. 817, 860 (1993).

27.   Eric J. Grannis, Note, *Fighting Words and Fighting Freestyle: The Constitutionality of Penalty Enhancement for Bias Crimes*, 93 COLUM. L. REV. 178, 230 (1993).

28.   Campos, *supra* note 26 at 849.

29.   Charles Fried, *Impudence*, SUP. CT. REV. 155, 167 (1992).

30.   For a useful discussion of resumptive, summative and free modifiers, see WILLIAMS, *supra* note 25, at 135-150.

31.   Cynthia G. Bowman, *Street Harassment and the Informal Ghettoization of Women*, 106 HARV L. REV. 517, 579. (1993).

32.   Burt Neuborne, *Of Sausage Factories and Syllogism Machines: Formalism, Realism, and Exclusionary Selection Techniques*, 67 N.Y.U. L. REV. 419, 421 (1992).

33.   Paulsen, *supra* note 15, at 1788.

34.   Stearns, *supra* note 3, at 515-16.

35.   *Id.*

36.   Clark D. Cunningham, *The Lawyer as Translator, Representation as Text: Towards an Ethnography of Legal Discourse*, 77 CORNELL L. REV. 1298, 1299 (1992).

37.   David L. Gregory, *Working for a Living*, 58 BROOK. L. REV. 1355, 1375 (1993) (book review).

38.   George D. Gopen *The State of Legal Writing: Res Ipsa Loquitur*, 86 MICH. L. REV. 333, 334 (1987).

39.   Starnes, *supra* note 9, at 70.

40.   Amar, *supra* note 18, at 759.

41.   HALL, *supra* note 1, at 27-28.

42.   *Id.*

43.   Stearns, *supra* note 3, at 514.

44.   Jerry Frug, *Decentering Decentralization*, 60 U. CHI. L. REV. 253 (1993).

45.   HALL, *supra* note 1, at 127.

46.   Ronald Dworkin, *Principle, Policy, Procedure*, in A MATTER OF PRINCIPLE 72 (1985).

47.   James B. White, *Judicial Criticism*, 20 GA. L. REV. 835, 837 (1986).

48.   Neuborne, *supra* note 32, at 420.

49.   RICHARD A. POSNER, THE PROBLEMS OF JURISPRUDENCE 233 (1990).

50.   Anthony G. Amsterdam, *Thurgood Marshall's Image of the Blue-eyed Child in* Brown 68 N.Y.U. L. REV. 226 (1993).

51.   RICHARD WEISBERG, POETHICS AND OTHER STRATEGIES OF LAW AND LITERATURE 217-18 (1992).

52.   PETER ELBOW, WRITING WITHOUT TEACHERS 39 (1973).

CHAPTER EIGHT

THE LAW REVIEW PROCESS:
EDITING THE WORK OF OTHERS

*"The essence of editing a law review is bringing out
the best each author has to offer. Although this may
sound simple, do not be deceived.... More than one
author has had chance to remark that it is the editor
who takes it upon himself to separate the wheat from
the chaff, and then prints the chaff."*
                                    - Michael J. Killeen

*"People ask you for criticism, but they only want
praise."*
                                    - Somerset Maugham

A law review editor is a gatekeeper and midwife. As a
gatekeeper, you must become familiar with your journal's publication
standards, its readership, and—if applicable—its particular focus or
slant, and then accept articles accordingly. As a midwife, your job
is to assist an author in delivering to the journal the best piece
possible. In this endeavor, you and the author are allies, not
adversaries—a divine state, if one fraught with peril. A productive
collaborative relationship is best maintained by sticking to the
editorial role—which is, experienced editors claim, "to bridge the gap
between the author's intention and the reader's understanding."[1]

Editors are not writers, not even ghostwriters. They do not make or alter meaning. They do not impose their style upon another. Rather they are intelligent, diligent, representative readers who can articulate what in the text might create a misunderstanding that diminishes the article's power and persuasiveness. Sometimes it takes a lot of work to figure out what is causing the confusion. Then it takes even more work to write out your thoughts in a clear and supportive manner. Editing a law review article is, therefore, surprisingly time-consuming and involves imagination, patience, tact, stress, and numerous phone calls and letters. And, after all this effort, do not expect to be universally appreciated. Authors, however seasoned and esteemed, tend to acknowledge constructive criticism mostly in retrospect.

This chapter is divided into three parts. We begin with some advice on article selection, continue with a description of the editing process, and conclude with a discussion on writing constructive comments.

A. GATEKEEPERS: ARTICLE SELECTION

Regardless of whether an article is written by an outside author or student author, publication decisions rest upon whether a piece contributes a new and significant insight into the law. The article must not involve dead or stale issues, nor should it pose questions the profession has already answered. The topic does not have to be "big," but it should be fresh, timely, and worthwhile.

Above and beyond topic and thesis, publication decisions depend upon an article's execution. Journals are plagued by "premature submissions,"[2] by authors who, in their rush to publish, fail to do the revision that turns a mere paper into a polished professional article. Whether the article is nonetheless worth considering depends on many factors, including your journal's reputation and the number of submissions it receives, as well as the author's stature and the type of substantive, stylistic, or organizational problems that exist.

Articles are rejected when reviewers, making a reasonable effort, cannot understand them. They are rejected when the piece fails to do what it says it is going to do, or when the writer's methods, examples, arguments, or sources are suspect. Some journals are reluctant to publish big "think" pieces or theory-building articles if authored by anyone less than a veteran in the field. Others may be inclined to reject articles when their tone is intemperate or insecure, when the style is turgid, or when the discussion wanders aimlessly. Nonetheless, it is rare to receive an article so perfect you can immediately put it into production. When the flaws are not fatal, the topic is ripe, the arguments cogent, the author august or promising, you may well want to extend an offer conditioned on revision.

When extending conditional offers, however, be very careful. Articles editors sometimes become so caught up in securing a promising article that a misunderstanding occurs about the journal's role in further work on that article. Sometimes authors expect the journal staff to function as an unnamed "co-author," doing more work than an editorial staff should or can do. Thus journal editors need to achieve a clear understanding with the author about what needs to be done to make the work publishable, and how much work the staff is willing and able to contribute.

Two last pieces of advice on article selection. You do not want to reject articles by "hot" authors, especially if you reject them unknowingly. Here are a few quick tricks law reviews use to check on authors and topics.

- Search the author's name in the LEXIS and WESTLAW law review databases. This will tell you whether the author has published recently in a prestigious journal. If so, check further to see which scholars are acknowledged in the author's footnotes.

- Benefit from your faculty advisor's "insider" experience by sending for review a weekly, or even daily, list of new submissions—authors and topics.

- And if the author is well-known, show administrative efficiency: phone to see if the article is still available and respond promptly if it is.

Finally, be sure to give less well-known authors a chance. It is often the newer members of the profession who are most attuned to new directions in the law.

In addition to selecting manuscripts from a pool of unsolicited submissions, solicitation of articles is an important part of putting together issues. In this respect, you may want to publish some theme issues in addition to any symposium issue that is scheduled. Theme issues enable you to interest well-known authors to write for your journal. Moreover, if you are fortunate enough to secure an article from someone prestigious, you can use that contribution to encourage articles from other respected authorities in that field. Less well-known journals often find this is an effective way to enhance their reputation in the legal community.

Theme issues can be important for another reason: they are widely read. Someone interested in a particular topic is more likely to pick up a volume devoted entirely to that subject than a volume with only one relevant article. Thus theme issues can be of special value for journals trying to expand their readership. Unless your journal is intended to be specialized, however, be careful not to devote too many issues to one area of the law. Variety also has its payoffs and is another way to ensure a broad audience.

B. MIDWIVES: STAGES IN THE EDITING PROCESS

The editing process tracks the writing process: just as a writer limits her concerns at each writing stage to avoid frustration and paralysis, so too an editor limits his area of concern so as to conserve energy and encourage, rather than discourage, the author.

The writing process tends to be a four-step process (reading and exploring, drafting, revising, polishing), and as primary editors of student articles, your editing will correspond to these four stages.[3] With student authors, the first two stages in both the writing and editing process are writer-based, that is, you and your editee focus on figuring out the problem. The second two stages are reader-based, that is, both parties focus on communicating the ideas to the article's intended audience. The editing process for outside authors should, presumably, be easier and shorter. These authors ought to have maneuvered through the early drafting stages on their own, and if they failed to do so, their articles do not merit serious consideration in your journal. At whichever stage you begin, keep in mind that although editing can be described as a four-stage process, one or all of the stages may need to be repeated: the analytic or organizational problems of an early draft may, for example, persist into later drafts and require you to repeat an earlier step.

1. *Beginning (The Reading and Exploring Stage)*

The editor's role at the beginning of the writing process is to help your editees narrow their topics and find a thesis. Your first major task is to make sure your editees have read widely enough that all brainstorming activities are situated within the general framework of literature on that topic. You do this to prevent writers from pursuing avenues already preempted or dismissed as irrelevant. Your second task is to assist your writers in "seeing" their own ideas. Be a second reader for your writers' reading journals and freewritings. Examine their case diagrams and issue trees. (See Chapters Two and Four.) As a reader with some distance on the subject, you may be able to notice themes, trends, and relations in your writers' raw materials that they overlooked. Say back to your writers what you hear them saying. Then ask questions about the topic that might help your writers hone their thinking, i.e., be a soundingboard for the writer's exploration.

2. *Drafting (Getting Ideas Down on Paper)*

By the drafting stage, the writer has articulated a thesis and is trying to get out the supporting arguments. The editor's primary role at this stage is to respond to the breadth, depth, development, originality, and credibility of those ideas. You should not worry at this point about their expression. Because the article is still in its childhood, and will develop in ways yet unknown, it is a waste of your energy and the author's emotions to perfect the material.

To generate comments on the viability and sufficiency of the analysis, to get a sense of the "Big Picture," try these techniques.

- Read through the entire draft without stopping. When you are finished, write down the thesis and the key arguments in support of the thesis. If you cannot do this successfully, it is likely that either the thesis or the arguments (or both) require clearer articulation.

- Outline the draft and then make notes about discrepancies, ambiguities, and digressions. Where is the analysis incomplete because of missing links in reasoning? Where is it unsupported? Where are there unhelpful digressions? Where is background needed?

- Read the article again, playing devil's advocate. Are the author's summaries of caselaw and secondary authority inaccurate? Did the author ignore seminal sources, depend on unreliable sources, or improperly document sources? Has the author overlooked crucial factual, doctrinal, or policy considerations? Has the author recognized and responded to opposing arguments? Are there logical mistakes—like confusing coincidental relationships with causal ones? Are the author's examples and illustrations ineffective?[4]

Once you have made notes on your observations, review your data. What does it amount to? What are the most serious problems? What is working out well? Write up your conclusions.

3. *Revising (Writing for Readers)*

Once the writer has a viable draft, both the editor and the author must turn their attention to the article's potential audience—to the reader. Here is where an editor can be of particular help to outside authors as well as student authors. As a careful reader who is especially knowledgeable about your journal's expectations, you are in a good position to notice both where the piece is difficult to follow and what has to be done to bring it up to publication standards. Your responses at this point should not center around the originality or credibility of the discussion (your central concerns in the first editing stages), but on how clearly the ideas are being communicated to the reader.

Here too it is helpful to make a topic sentence outline that will assist you in getting an overview of organizational and substantive problems. Ask yourself these questions.

<u>Organization</u>

- Did outlining become difficult at any point? Did you encounter places where you wondered whether an idea was subissue B or issue II?

- Did the writer move from what the reader knows (old information) to what the reader doesn't know (new information)?

- Are the issues in order of importance? Is that order logical?

- Are the issues clearly separated or are some blurred together?

- Is the organization of each section internally logical?

- Does each section have its own introduction and conclusion?

- Are there topic and transition sentences?

Substance

- Would a reader benefit from additional background or reasoning?

- Are there still digressions?

- Do terms need to be defined?

- Is there too much or too little detail?

You should also raise the following questions in order to sensitize your editee to the rhetorical situation—to the article's purpose, audience, and tone.

Rhetorical Considerations

- Do the article's introduction and conclusion reflect the same purpose? Should either or both be changed to better reflect what the author has actually done?

- Is the paper responsive to the needs and expertise of a law-school-educated reader? Does it properly balance how much information readers have against how much they need?

- Has the author established an appropriate tone? Is it consistently maintained or does the author inappropriately lapse into sarcasm, anger, or timidity?

After asking these questions, review their import and write up your conclusions.

4. *Polishing*

By the time you arrive at the fourth stage, the paper is just about finished. The last step is to remove all the surface glitches to ensure a pleasurable reading experience. Your key job here is to catch all the mechanical errors and awkward expressions.

Although you have already commented on topic and transition sentences, check them again. In addition, examine paragraphs for unity and cohesion. Is there more than one idea in a paragraph? If so, divide it. Are the sentences in the right order? If not, re-order. Are the connections between sentences clear? If not, add transition words and use dovetailing. (See Chapter Five, Part E.)

Spend some time thinking about the author's writing style. Some writers might adopt a rather conversational tone while others have a formal tone. Such choices are an author's to make. But you should comment on any stylistic traits that interfere with comprehension. Does the author use clear sentence structures? Vary sentence length? Use language precisely and appropriately? (See Chapter Seven and Appendix A.)

Finally, correct mechanical errors—that is, errors in grammar, punctuation, quotation, and citation—and proofread for typographical mistakes. (See Appendices B and D.) To aid your concentration when proofreading, copy editors suggest (1) that you read the pages of a document out of order or backwards, (2) that you move a ruler under each line as you read, (3) that you doublecheck cross references, words in a different typeface, and names, titles, and numbers in footnotes, (4) that you search for the second half of quotation marks, brackets, parentheses, and dashes, and (5) that you check headings for consistency of formatting and agreement with the table of contents.[5]

Line editing is appropriate at this stage, but you may want to write some overall comments if you think there are some persistent problems on the paragraph or sentence level that the writer needs to address throughout the text.

C. WRITING CONSTRUCTIVE COMMENTS

1. *Editing Protocol*

Most authors harbor fantasies of an editor saying: "This piece is dazzling. I could not think of a single suggestion for revision." But, in reality, such a response is not likely, nor is it truly expected. As long as you take a writer seriously, and word your recommendations courteously, most authors put on a brave face and react positively.

The first maxim when it comes to writing up your appraisal is always to temper criticism with praise. An entirely negative critique is demoralizing and counter-productive. If you point out the strengths of the article, you are not only helping the writer to recognize your standards, but you may be dissipating antagonism and resistance.

The second maxim is to focus your comments on the article's future readers and on the article itself, instead of on the writer's performance.[6] In other words, do not focus on the mistake, shift the focus to the effect the mistake will have on the reader's reaction or understanding. Do not write: "You have taken a consistently patronizing tone." Instead, write: "Our readers might find this passage overly simplified; perhaps you should up the ante." It is always a good idea to re-read your comments, trying to hear them from the writer's point-of-view.

The third maxim is do not edit what you do not have to, i.e., do not step over the line by usurping the writer's role. It is the author's job to determine the content and to set the tone (as long as it does not antagonize the reader)—not the editor's job. It is especially important to be tactful and circumspect when editing outside authors. They have, after all, greater legal expertise than law review editors and probably more writing experience as well. Although they are likely to give your suggestions mature consideration, they are also in a better position than a second-year student to evaluate your own evaluation and to take it on *its* merits. Be, therefore, thoughtful and diplomatic.

2. *Types of Feedback*

When you write up your comments, you should be aware that there are different types of feedback—exploratory, descriptive, prescriptive, and judgmental.[7] Your comments should ultimately be a combination of all four. Although these different types of responses are all helpful to a writer, some may be more appropriate at one stage in the editing process than at another.

a. *Exploratory Feedback*

Exploratory feedback is especially helpful in the earlier stages of writing. By raising interpretations, meanings, choices, and strategies other than those presented in the draft, the editor helps the writer to explore the problem thoroughly and to refine her thesis. Exploratory feedback is collaborative brainstorming; it prevents premature thesis selection and simplistic analysis. Although exploratory feedback leads writers to the missing evidence and analysis that would improve the work, it is neither prescriptive nor judgmental.

b. *Descriptive Feedback*

When an editor reacts as a reader and describes as neutrally as possible her reactions to the text, she is providing descriptive feedback. An editee needs to know how a reader reacts to the text in order to determine whether the text accurately and easily communicated the writer's ideas to the reader or whether revision is needed. Although descriptive feedback is non-judgmental, since it simply reflects the meaning that was conveyed, it also prepares the ground for revision. Descriptive feedback is helpful in the early and late stages of writing.

c. *Prescriptive Feedback*

Prescriptive feedback is based on the editor's diagnosis of the cause of ineffectiveness. It offers suggestions on how to revise. It is sometimes difficult to decide how directive or non-directive to be. Your decision will probably depend on the editee. For some, especially outside authors, strategy-provoking questions will be enough for a writer to figure out what to do next. For others, explicit instructions might be necessary.

d. Judgmental Feedback

An editor must eventually offer an opinion on the quality of the writing submitted. Outside articles must be selected or rejected. New journal members need to know how close or far they are from producing a publishable piece of work. But, to be fair, editees need to be exposed to professional standards early enough in the writing process that they may identify their proficiencies and deficiencies and improve their skills. Thus, editors must articulate their standards, realizing that

- judgments should be based on shared, objective criteria;

- judgments should be geared to the particular stage of the writing process (first drafts should not be judged by the same standards as final drafts);

- judgments should be positive as well as negative; and

- judgments should be impersonal, not personal; they should be couched in terms of the document and the journal's needs, not in terms of the writer's abilities.

———

In the edit that follows, we annotate an editor's comments on an article on loss of consortium in wrongful death actions to show how these different types of feedback mingle. The comments were offered while the writer was in the early stages of drafting.

<u>Sample Critique (Early Stage)</u>

This draft shows the depth and breadth of your research...you probably don't need to do much more. Moreover, between the footnotes and the text, the draft is chockful of ideas (*positive feedback*). Nonetheless, the note is still descriptive, not analytic. Your very organization reflects this: you have an introduction, followed by three summaries and a conclusion. First, you summarize the general development of the wrongful death action, then its development in New York, then its status in other states. You do not even have an analysis section; rather you move directly into your conclusion. You have a point of view, but you do not have clear arguments in support of it (*primarily descriptive feedback*).

You have a couple of options in rethinking and rewriting your note. Your analysis could be organized around the arguments in support of recovery for loss of consortium. Much of your research is usable, but raise cases cited in support of arguments rather than in an historical narrative. (Note that many arguments are implicit in your footnotes.)

*   the illogic of allowing recovery in personal injury but not wrongful death
*   the illogic of allowing children recovery for loss of services but not spouses (see footnote 10 & page 17)
*   the general willingness of the judiciary to act in tort areas (give other examples in this cause of action [see footnote #23] and others)
*   social changes that dictate a new policy
*   trends in related causes of action and allied areas

You could narrow your topic to some of the problems that may have retarded recovery and try to pose solutions.

*   what courts have done in other instances of legislative inaction
*   difficulty in calculating damages (although this is a bit of a straw man argument)
*   concern about excessive damages (page 21)
*   how to handle claims for loss of consortium when the marriage is incompatible (fn 38)

You could focus on what a valid test for determining damages might be, as you start on page 13 (*primarily exploratory feedback*).

Obviously when you find your angle, you will need to rethink the sections of your note. In writing each section, remember to begin with an introductory thesis paragraph. Your reader will find it much easier to follow your points if the text has introductory paragraphs that establish the context and foreshadow the discussion (*prescriptive feedback*).

Overall, good start. But to be published, you still need to decide on *one* angle and then pursue it singlemindedly (*prescriptive and judgmental*).

3. *Organizing Your Comments*

Law review editors are notoriously fond of line edits, and indeed, there is a time and place for those. Line edits are never, however, a replacement for "global," big-picture comments. Marginal comments are rarely absorbed with the same ease as overall comments, nor are they credited with the same seriousness. Nor can you routinely substitute conversation for a letter or memo. Some of your finest perceptions may be forgotten when the telephone receiver is replaced or door closed. Thus, you should give your editees a written assessment of their work.

Moreover, if you want your editees truly to benefit from your comments, and to incorporate them into their rewrites, you must organize your critique. A critique that is stream-of-consciousness is probably as confusing as an article that is stream-of-consciousness—and will likely produce a rewrite that is differently but equally stream-of-consciousness.

How you organize your comments depends on where you are in the editing process and what problems exists. In the beginning, you may want to write *overall comments* that are directed to the *analytic substance* of the piece, to its focus (thesis) and scope (arguments). Later, you may want to add a section on *large-scale organization*—where you discuss the division of arguments, the order of arguments, the separation of issues and subissues, and the presence of introductions and conclusions. If there are persistent problems with paragraphing, syntax, diction, or mechanics, you may want from the beginning to include a *writing* section so that certain mistakes are not carried through draft after draft. Otherwise, you may leave this for later edits, or for a line edit.

When you are further along in the process, you might want to comment on each part of the article separately—focusing in turn on the content, analysis, and large- and small-scale organization of each section, as well as on paragraphing and prose.

What follows is, we think, a thorough, well organized, thoughtful critique of an article in the later stages of development. You can play with and adapt its format until you find one with which you are comfortable. In addition to its encouraging tone, note especially the specificity of its description of problems and of its suggested solutions.

Sample Critique (Revision Stage)

This piece is beautifully written, very interesting and on a timely topic. Nonetheless, as this memo describes, I have several suggestions that I hope will make it even stronger.

I.   Synthesis

In a significant way, the paper reads like two different pieces. The problem results, I think, from your analytic framework. Sections IV A & B have too few over-arching ideas; in short, both sections should be subsets of a larger analytical whole.

Thus, I suggest you edit each section with an eye toward highlighting the common themes in the sections themselves and in the introduction. For example, section A's discussion of the retrenchment of rights in <u>Oliver</u> and <u>Burger</u> makes for easy cross reference as part of B's discussion of the history of the new federalism, i.e., as examples of Supreme Court restriction of federal constitutional rights that inspired state Supreme Courts to give teeth to state constitutional provisions.

II.   Section A

A couple of points here. First, an observation in regard to references to the fourth amendment. Since the fourth amendment itself recognizes and balances the interests of individual rights with society's interest in crime prevention (in proscribing unreasonable searches and seizures), a statement like "<u>Burger</u>'s central concern...is efficient law enforcement, not the fourth amendment" is not quite right. Concern for law enforcement is not trumping the fourth amendment, it is trumping individual rights. The criticism is where the Court draws the line between the competing values inherent in the fourth.

Second, some readers might find your treatment of Powell "unfair." Powell, though concededly pro-government on criminal matters, on a variety of civil cases is famous for concurrences in 4-4 splits where he agonizes over the precedents, searching for a principled way out. Thus, the following statement is too sweeping: "For Justice Powell, any two assertions of the Court's authority are inherently consistent."

Nonetheless, this section works; it has several keen insights.

III.   Section B

This section might benefit from some reorganization. My suggested organization of this section is as follows:

i.   Introduction of New Federalism. Here give history: incorporation doctrine, expansion of federal rights and application to actions by state government, retrenchment, the Brennan and Marshall dissents calling state courts to action, the S.Ct. response and changed presumption under adequate state ground doctrine.

ii.   Then give arguments on both sides, including discussion of Gardner now on p. 95.

iii.   Then, as an example of how one court has gone, insert discussion of New Jersey opinions here.

iv.   Finally, in distinction to how N.J. got it right, show how N.Y. got it wrong.

Again, despite these suggestions, this section is a strong contribution to moving the debate forward in a fascinating area. The article is very promising.

Please call me with any questions you have about these comments.

NOTES

1.   Sheila Barrows, *Establishing Collaborative Author/Editor Relationships: The Heldref Paradigm in* WRITING AND PUBLISHING FOR ACADEMIC AUTHORS 289 (Joseph M. Moxley, ed. 1992).

2.   Gary A. Olson coins this phrase in *Publishing Scholarship in Humanistic Disciplines: Joining the Conversation*, *in* WRITING AND PUBLISHING, *supra* note 1, at 61.

3.   We are indebted to Jessie Grearson, John Marshall Law School, for sending us materials from her presentation to the SOFTWARE LAW JOURNAL that outlined the four steps in editing that we recommend here. For a discussion of how these four steps relate to the writing process in general, see Jessie Grearson, *Process to Product: Teaching the Writing Process in Law School*, 9 THE SECOND DRAFT 1 (1993).

4.   Anne Enquist, *After the Fact Outlines: An Old Idea Put to New Use*, 6 WASH. ENG. J. (1984) at 29. We are also grateful to Anne for sending us unpublished materials on law review editing that included these editing techniques.

5.   For more on copy editing, see Carolyn B. Bagin & Jo Van Doren, *Everyone is a Proofreader: How to Check Your Documents*, *in* WRITING AND PUBLISHING, *supra* note 1, at 261-64.

6.   Mary B. Ray & Jill J. Ramsfield make this very sensible suggestion in LEGAL WRITING: GETTING IT RIGHT AND GETTING IT WRITTEN 89 (2nd ed. 1993).

7.   Kristin Woolever & Brook K. Baker, *Diagnosing Legal Writing Problems: Theoretical and Practical Perspectives for Giving Feedback*, Panel Presentation at the Legal Writing Institute Conference, Ann Arbor, Michigan, July 28, 1990.

APPENDIX A

GRAMMAR AND USAGE

Appendix B on punctuation and this appendix review some of the basic principles and prescriptions of standard written American English. This review is not intended as a substitute for a good basic text or reference book, however. Every writer's permanent library should include at least one grammar and one usage book like those on the reading list at the end of Chapter Five.

A few of the topics in these appendices are "musts": to violate them is to do serious injustice to your ideas. Sentences must have a subject and a predicate, subject and verb must "agree" in person and number, nouns and pronouns must "agree," verb tenses must be appropriate, and modifiers and modified must be rationally related. We also consider the use of inclusive rather than sexist language an imperative. For the rest, though, as you will see, we prefer sensible flexibility to rigid rules. Our aim here is to provide you with a vocabulary for articulating your own and your editees' writing problems. Once you have a diagnosis, revision is easier. The last entry in this appendix, Editors' Abbreviations, provides a useful shorthand for indicating errors and problems.

AGREEMENT: SUBJECT/VERB AND PRONOUN/ANTECEDENT

Subjects and verbs must agree in number—that is, singular subjects go with singular verbs and plural subjects go with plural verbs.

Ex: The fifth amendment guarantees due process of law.

Ex: The fifth and fourteenth amendments guarantee due process of law.

Most of the time, compliance with this basic rule is automatic. Writers nonetheless get into trouble in a few situations. For example, when a sentence becomes very complex, it is easy to lose track of the subject, as did the writer in the example below.

Not: Some commentators have argued that *the venerable history and principled rationale* supporting the exercise of peremptory challenges by the defense in a criminal prosecution, particularly in view of the heterogeneous nature of our society, *outweighs* the individual juror's right to serve on a given case.

Confusion also occurs when a singular subject is followed by prepositional phrases like "together with," and "in addition to." Remember that unlike conjunctions, these phrases do not make a plural verb form necessary.

Ex: Its venerable history *and* principled rationale *outweigh* other considerations. (Conjunction; plural verb form.)
Ex: Its venerable history, *together with* its principled rationale, *outweighs* other considerations. (Prepositional phrase; singular verb form.)

Other problems arise with collective nouns like "government," "corporation," or "jury" used as subjects. Traditional legal usage treats most of these as singular.

Ex: The jury deliberates in secret.
Ex: The government has fewer peremptory challenges.

Pronouns and their "antecedents"—the words they replace—must agree in gender and number. Agreement is basic and automatic—and also the occasion of many errors. As with subject/verb agreement, collective nouns are troublesome. In general, they need the singular neuter pronoun "it."

Ex: The jury rendered *its* verdict and the court *its* judgment.

But the most frequent error is the use of the third-person plural pronouns "they," "them," and "their" with singular antecedents—for example, "A person is responsible for the foreseeable consequences of their actions." This usage arises from the commendable attempt to avoid both sexism ("his") and awkwardness ("his or her"), but despite its growing acceptance in speech and very informal writing, this use of plural pronouns is inappropriate in scholarly writing. (See "Avoiding Sexist Language," below.)

AVOIDING SEXIST LANGUAGE

Perhaps the hardest part of writing sexist language out of our prose is avoiding the "generic" use of the pronouns "he," "him," and "his."*

<u>Not</u>:   A judge must try to put *his* personal biases aside.

Some common solutions follow.

● Make the *noun* plural. (Using a plural pronoun with a singular noun is not appropriate in scholarly writing.)

<u>Ex</u>:   Judges must try to set their personal biases aside.

<u>Not</u>:   A judge must try to set their personal biases aside.

● Omit the pronoun.

<u>Ex</u>:   A judge must try to set personal biases aside.

● Use "a," "an," "the," "any."

<u>Ex</u>:   A judge must set any personal biases aside.

● Use "who."

<u>Ex</u>:   A judge who has personal biases must set them aside.

● Use "one," "you," or "we."

<u>Ex</u>:   As judges, we must set our personal biases aside.

---

* The problem is that "he," like "man," is never really gender-neutral. This is why we find "irredeemably odd" the sentences "Each applicant is to list the name of his husband or wife" and "Some men are female." Moreover, empirical evidence suggests that the generic "he" is in fact perceived by readers as male; thus footnotes to the effect that the writers use "he" to refer to both males and females are futile gestures despite the best of intentions. *See* Virginia L. Warren, *Guidelines for Non-Sexist Use of Language*, 59 AM. PHIL. ASS'N. PROC. 471 (1986).

When all else fails, and only when all else fails, rewrite in the passive voice or resort to "he or she," "his or her," etc.

When writing a long document where the pronoun problem is endemic, some writers choose to alternate "he" and "she" or use "she" alone to heighten the reader's awareness of the issue. These are more controversial solutions, however.

BEGINNING SENTENCES: *AND, BUT,* AND *BECAUSE*

Some writers and editors believe that it is incorrect to start a sentence with "and," "but," or "because." Although they may perhaps strike a too casual note in contracts or wills, we believe that "and," "but," and "because" are entirely acceptable sentence openers in scholarly writing. Indeed, they sound less stilted than their fancy equivalents "additionally," "however," and "since."

COMPLEX SUBJECTS

Long, abstract subjects make sentences difficult to understand.

> <u>Not</u>: *The government's use of sophisticated technology to reconstruct evidence of criminal activity found in trash discarded in a publicly accessible place* does not violate the fourth amendment.

In the example above, the reader trudges through a complicated and depopulated twenty-one-word subject—composed of one main noun ("use") and its modifiers—in order to reach the verb. The message in this sentence can be conveyed more effectively by using a short subject that is the agent of the action.

> <u>Ex</u>: *The government* does not violate the fourth amendment when it uses sophisticated technology to reconstruct evidence of criminal activity found in trash that has been discarded in a publicly accessible place.

INTERRUPTING CLAUSES AND PHRASES

Long or habitual interruptions between subject and verb most often confuse and frustrate the reader.

> <u>Not</u>: *The Supreme Court,* which had earlier held in *Engel* and subsequently in *Lee* that state-sponsored prayer in public schools has an inescapably coercive effect on children who do not

wish, for whatever reason, to participate, nonetheless *denied* certiorari.

Yet interruption can sometimes be used to good effect for emphasis or cadence. In the following passage from his dissent in an affirmative action case, Justice Blackmun uses interruptions to make his point.

> I never thought that I would live to see the day when the city of Richmond, Virginia, the cradle of the Old Confederacy, sought on its own, within a narrow confine, to lessen the stark impact of persistent discrimination. But Richmond, to its great credit, acted. Yet this Court, the supposed bastion of equality, strikes down Richmond's efforts....

MODIFIERS: MISPLACED AND DANGLING

Misplaced and dangling modifiers are inevitable in first drafts. If they are not fixed at the revision stage, however, they make our prose look slipshod. Always keep modifiers close to what they modify. When modifiers stray, confusion and incongruity follow, as in the example below, where the writer unwittingly gives new meaning to the term "contempt of court."

> <u>Not</u>: *Even when they are mechanically shredded*, the federal courts will not find a reasonable expectation of privacy in *discarded documents*.

> <u>Ex</u>: The federal courts will not find a reasonable expectation of privacy in *discarded documents, even when they are mechanically shredded.*

More difficult to diagnose and fix than misplaced modifiers are "dangling" modifiers. They "dangle" because there is in fact nothing for them to modify, nothing in the sentence to which they can properly attach themselves.

> <u>Not</u>: *Citing the first amendment*, the injunction was dismissed. (The injunction did not cite the first amendment, a court did.)

The simplest way to correct the example above would be to insert the word being modified—"the court."

> <u>Ex</u>: Citing the first amendment, the court dismissed the injunction.

NOMINALIZATIONS

"Nominalizations" are nouns formed from verbs. For example, "reversal" comes from the verb "to reverse" and "collision" from "to collide." Your prose will be stronger and more direct if you habitually use verbs, and not their nominalizations.

> <u>Not</u>:   The planes were involved in a mid-air collision.

> <u>Ex</u>:   The planes collided in mid-air.

You should note, however, that nominalizations are not always inappropriate. They can lend formality to your prose and they can be useful in parallel construction (see below) and in dovetailing sentences (see Chapter 5, Part E).

PARALLEL CONSTRUCTION

When items in pairs or series are "parallel"—all in the same grammatical category (e.g., nouns, infinitives, past participles) —sentences are balanced and readable. Verb tenses should be consistent, and if the conjunction "that" introduces one item in a series, it should introduce all.

> <u>Ex</u>:   Plaintiff challenges the Pledge-recitation statute, arguing 1) that its plain meaning violates the free speech clause, 2) that recitation of the phrase "under God" violates the establishment clause, and 3) that recitation by teachers and willing pupils unconstitutionally coerces children who do not wish to pledge.

> <u>Not</u>:   Plaintiff challenges the Pledge-recitation statute, arguing 1) that the free speech clause was violated, 2) reciting the phrase "under God" violates the establishment clause, and 3) children who do not wish to pledge are unconstitutionally coerced by recitation by teachers and willing pupils.

Faulty parallelism makes the second example hard to read. The writer uses "that" in only one of three items, uses both passive and active voice, uses past and present tenses, and uses the noun "recitation" and the participle "reciting."

PASSIVE V. ACTIVE VOICE

Prose in which the active voice predominates is generally clearer and stronger than prose that relies on the passive voice. In the active voice, the grammatical subject of the sentence is the agent of the action.

> Ex: The defendant breached his duty of care.

In the passive voice, however, the grammatical subject of the sentence is not the agent of the action, but rather, the person or thing acted upon. Indeed, the agent of the action need not appear in the sentence at all.

> Ex: The duty of care was breached.

The passive voice is most appropriate when the agent of the action is understood, or when the agent is unknown.

> Ex: The judgment was reversed.

> Ex: The building was vandalized.

The passive voice is also useful in dovetailing your sentences into a cohesive paragraph. (See Chapter 5, Part E.)

SENTENCE COHERENCE: USING THE RIGHT WORD

When writers are in a hurry to get their ideas down on paper, they often write incoherent sentences. They yoke inappropriate verbs to their subjects and create apples-and-oranges comparisons. Enhancing sentence coherence is an important goal of the revising and editing processes.

> Not: The Court also felt that gender-based challenges to jurors could be used as a pretext for racist challenges.

> Not: Like *Barnette*, the court held that no one should be compelled to recite the Pledge of Allegiance.

Note how in the first example above, the use of the vague, "grab-bag" verb "felt" blurs meaning. (Was the Court reasoning? Expressing apprehension? Expressing approval?) In the second sentence, a decision is inappropriately compared to a court.

SPLIT INFINITIVES

Careful writers apply a presumption against splitting infinitives (putting an adverb after the "to").

    <u>Not</u>:   It is the court's task to judiciously balance the equities.

In the example above, the adverb can easily be moved.

    <u>Ex</u>:   It is the court's task to balance the equities judiciously.

But always begin by asking yourself whether you really need the offending adverb. In the example above, "judiciously" is redundant. How else should a court balance equities?

The presumption against splitting infinitives is overcome when placement of the adverb elsewhere in the sentence creates ambiguity or the adverb and verb are frequent companions.

    <u>Ex</u>:   The failure to properly acknowledge sources exposes a writer to charges of plagiarism.

In the example above, "properly" cannot follow "sources" without creating ambiguity ("properly exposes"). Moreover, when "to properly acknowledge" is translated into an adjective-noun pair, the result is "proper acknowledgment," a common expression.

THAT **OR** *WHICH?*

The relative pronouns "that" and "which" are the subject of confusion among writers and controversy among editors. "That" is used only to introduce restrictive clauses—clauses intrinsic to a sentence's message—and does not properly begin a non-restrictive, incidental clause. Only "which" properly introduces a non-restrictive clause. (Remember that non-restrictive clauses are set off by commas, as though between parentheses.)

    <u>Ex</u>:   The issue *that* divided the court most bitterly was capital punishment. (restrictive)

    <u>Ex</u>:   The issue, *which* divided the court most bitterly, was whether execution constitutes cruel and unusual punishment. (non-restrictive)

Many writers use "which" interchangeably with "that" in restrictive clauses.

    <u>Ex</u>:   The issue *which* divided the court most bitterly was capital punishment.

Others, known to the less zealous as "which-hunters," insist that only "that" is correct in restrictive clauses. We believe both are acceptable in scholarly writing. However, where the confusion of restrictive with non-restrictive language would be consequential, use "that" to introduce restrictive clauses. (See Appendix B, Commas, below.)

VERB TENSES

Always use the past tense to relate the facts of the case.

> Ex: The suspect fled from the scene, but was arrested two months later. Charged with murder, he pled guilty.

Always use the past perfect to describe the earlier of two past actions.

> Ex: The suspect *had disappeared* by the time the police arrived at the scene.

The "historical present" is not ordinarily appropriate in scholarly writing.

> Not: The suspect flees from the scene, but is arrested two months later. Charged with murder, he pleads guilty.

However, the present tense *is* appropriate when you are describing a court's reasoning, although the past tense may also be used.

> Ex: The majority analogizes gender-based discrimination to race-based discrimination. The dissent, however, distinguishes between the two.

WHO OR *WHOM?*

The rules governing the use of this fiendish pair of pronouns are easy to state, but difficult to apply. Careful writers use "whom" when the pronoun is 1) the object of a preposition, 2) the object of a verb, or 3) the subject of an infinitive. "Who" is appropriate when the pronoun is 1) the subject of any verb form except an infinitive, or 2) the subject of a subjective complement. Problems arise because it is not always easy to tell whether the pronoun functions as subject or object. It helps to take the troublesome clause out of its context, rearrange it in normal subject-verb-object order, and substitute a personal pronoun for who/m. If a subject pronoun—"I," "we," "he," "she," or "they"—seems appropriate, use "who." If an object pronoun—"me," "us," "him," "her," "them"—sounds more natural, use "whom."

> Ex: Justice Holmes is a jurist *about whom much has already been written*. (object of the preposition "about") (much has already been written about *him*)

> Ex: The suspects *whom the police arrested* were questioned. (object of the verb "arrested") (the police arrested *them*)

> Ex: *Whom do we want to interpret* our Constitution? (subject of the infinitive "to interpret") (we want *them* to interpret)

> Ex: Police officers may not arrest just anyone *who they think committed a crime*. (subject of the verb "committed") (they think *she* committed a crime)

> Ex: The perpetrator was not the man *who they thought he was*. (subject of a subjective complement) (they thought it was *he*)

Finally, if nothing seems to help, do what experienced writers do: rewrite the sentence to eliminate the problem who/m.

WORDINESS: DIAGNOSIS AND CURE**

Wordiness is something we all know when we see it. But the simple marginal comment "wordy" rarely serves writer or editor well; it is a general description of a writing problem, not a precise diagnosis. A line-edit may solve the immediate problem, but it will not help the writer. Take, for example, the sentence below.

> In general, the end result of the correction of any and all errors of substance, organization, grammar, usage, spelling, and punctuation that may have been made by the author will be an article, note, or comment that is excellent with respect to quality and an author who, it is fair to say, is desirous of implementing a homicidal design upon the person of the editor.

We can all agree that this sentence is unacceptably "wordy." But what makes it that way?

**   The discussion that follows is inspired in part by JOSEPH M. WILLIAMS' excellent section on the causes and cures of wordiness in Chapter 7 of STYLE: TOWARD CLARITY AND GRACE (1990).

Wordiness is really a constellation of bad writing habits, the most common of which are the following.

1) The use of complex subjects. (See above, "Complex Subjects.")

2) The use of compound prepositions.

3) The use of nominalizations instead of verbs. (See above, "Nominalizations.")

4) The utilization of jargon and pompous legalese.

5) The use of redundant pairs. English has these in abundance—for example, "one and only," "basic and fundamental," "any and all."

6) The use of unnecessary categories—for example, "green in color," "the crime of homicide."

7) Redundant or meaningless modifiers—for example, "personal belongings," "past history."

8) Meaningless "throat-clearing" phrases—for example, "on the whole."

9) Elaborating on the obvious.

10) Piling on unnecessary detail.

11) Using "of" to express possession—for example, "the extent of the responsibility of appellate counsel."

12) Over-use of writing about writing, called "metadiscourse"—for example, "This paper will now discuss in turn each prong of the three-prong test."

With this in mind, we can diagnose the example above.

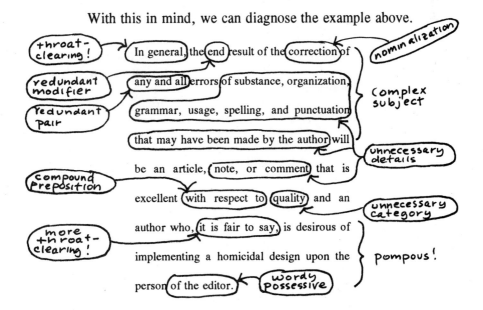

With all of the various kinds of wordiness removed, this sentence might read:

> The correction of all of the author's errors will result
> in an excellent article and a homicidal author.

Finally, we could improve our rewrite further by making an "actor" in the story the subject of the sentence and using the verb "to correct" instead of the nominalization "correction."

> If you correct all your author's mistakes, you will have
> an excellent article and a homicidal author.

EDITORS' ABBREVIATIONS

sp.	Spelling error	r-o	Run-on sentence
w.w.	Wrong word	n/pro.	Noun-pronoun agreement
m.m.	Misplaced Modifier	s/v agr.	Subject-verb agreement
d.m.	Dangling modifier	ref?	Pronoun reference unclear
frag.	Sentence fragment	coh.	Coherence
a.v.	Use active voice	llism	Use parallel construction

APPENDIX B

PUNCTUATION

A. PUNCTUATION STYLES

This appendix is not a complete guide to punctuation; it focuses on the most basic rules and those most often broken.

Preliminarily, though, a few words about rules and styles are in order. There are two basic styles of punctuation, "tight" and "loose." Tight punctuation follows all of the rules all of the time. Loose punctuation distinguishes between optional and mandatory rules and even condones occasional violations of mandatory rules in the service of personal style. Tight punctuation is a tool of precision, and is therefore required in instrumental legal writing, especially in private and public rule-making prose: statutes, regulations, wills, contracts, and leases. Loose punctuation is often used in informal letters, in fiction or personal essays, and in journalism. What style of punctuation is appropriate for scholarly legal writing? A casenote or seminar paper is at once more personal than a contract and more formal than a short story. It is our view that as a scholarly writer, you can never go wrong by following all of the rules of punctuation all of the time. We also believe, however, that as an editor, you can be *too* zealous. Where an author has punctuated loosely, and that style does not compromise clarity, we would require only consistency. Of course, your journal may have a strict house style that leaves editors no choice. Where the choice is yours, however, we urge respect for the writer's own style. The discussion that follows will indicate which rules are optional in a loose punctuation style. Tight punctuation style requires you to observe all of the rules below.

B. PERIODS

Put a period at the end of a sentence—and nowhere else. In other words, avoid both run-on sentences and sentence fragments. At a minimum, a sentence consists of a subject and a predicate and expresses a complete thought. For example, the simple sentence "The witness testified" is composed of a subject (the witness) and a predicate (testified) and expresses a complete thought. Most sentences also need a complement to finish the thought begun by the subject and predicate: "The discovery rule is *an equitable doctrine.*"

Two complete sentences incorrectly joined by a comma create a variety of run-on sentence sometimes called a "comma-splice."

> <u>Not</u>:   The discovery rule is an equitable doctrine, its purpose
> is to do justice between the parties.

There are three ways to correct this comma-splice: by replacing the comma with a period, by replacing it with a semicolon, or by adding a coordinating conjunction after the comma (here "and" is the obvious choice).

Although run-on sentences should always be avoided, good writers sometimes deliberately use sentence fragments, for emphasis or to surprise the reader.

> <u>Ex</u>:   Perhaps these proposals, so contrary to the established
> approach, come too early. Or too late.

C. COMMAS

1.   Put a comma after an introductory word, phrase, or dependent clause.

> <u>Ex</u>:   During the past several terms, the Court has had ample
> opportunities to revisit the issue.

> <u>Ex</u>:   If the jury had been properly instructed, it would have
> acquitted the defendant.

However, when the introduction consists of a word or very short phrase, loose punctuation omits this comma.

> <u>Ex</u>:   Today the courts approach the issue differently.

2.   Put a comma, called the "serial comma," between all items in a series of three or more.   Loose punctuation omits the comma that precedes the "and," but the better practice is to use it, because it can resolve ambiguities.   Note that without the final comma, it would be unclear in the example below whether "the latter" refers to "services" or "goods and services."

> Ex: Real property, securities, and goods and services were all involved, particularly the latter.

3.   Put a comma between two independent clauses joined by a coordinating conjunction (and, but, or, nor, for, so, yet).   An independent clause has a subject and predicate and could stand alone as a sentence.   When the clauses are short, loose punctuation omits this comma.

> Ex: No arrests or prosecutions under the statute occurred, and the union and the employer eventually resolved their dispute.

> Ex: Negotiations broke down and the union struck.

You should note that "however" and "therefore" are *not* coordinating conjunctions and cannot be used with a comma to join two independent clauses.   Only a semicolon is correct in that situation.

> Not: The district court concluded that the statute was constitutional, however, the court of appeals reversed.

> Ex: The district court concluded that the statute was constitutional; however, the court of appeals reversed.

4.   Use a comma (or commas) to set off a phrase or clause that is interrupting or "non-restrictive"—that is, when it provides information inessential to our understanding of the main clause.   Do not use a comma if the information is essential—if the phrases or clause is "restrictive."   (For the proper use of "that" and "which," see Appendix A.)

> Ex: The testator left his assets, which were in Utah, to his wife. (Non-restrictive: assets incidently located in Utah.)

> Ex: The testator left to his wife his assets that were in Utah. (Restrictive: *only* those assets in Utah.)

5. Do *not* put a comma between subject and verb.   The temptation to make this mistake most often arises in a sentence that

is top-heavy with an overly complex subject.   (See Appendix A, Complex Subjects.)

> Not: *The principle of the existence of a reasonable expectation of privacy in documents shredded into small pieces by the defendant prior to disposal*, was traditionally assumed by the courts.

   6.   Put a comma before a phrase tacked on to a sentence like an afterthought.

> Ex: The negotiations were prolonged, not to mention vehement.

D. SEMICOLONS

   1.   Use semicolons in a list of three or more items if one or more of the items contains an internal comma.

> Ex: The court weighs such factors as distance from the home itself; efforts, if any, to screen the area from view; and the type, frequency, and duration of occupation.

   2.   Use a semicolon to join two independent clauses, especially when you wish to connect or contrast their meanings. This is one way to correct the run-on caused by a comma splice. You must be certain, however, that *both* clauses could stand alone as complete sentences.

> Ex: This decision is both edifying and cautionary; it simultaneously shows the court at its best and at its worst.

> Not: This decision is both edifying and cautionary; the court at its best and at its worst.

E. COLONS

Use a colon to introduce a list if what precedes the list could stand on its own as a complete sentence.

> Ex: Non-interpretive factors include the following: pre-existing common-law, legislative history, and local custom.

> Not: Non-interpretive factors include: pre-existing common-law, legislative history, and local custom.

A colon is also used to introduce a formal question, quotation, amplification, or example.

> Ex: The discovery rule is an equitable doctrine: a way to do justice between the parties.

F. DASHES

Use a long dash ("em dash") or two short dashes to set off interrupting or other non-restrictive information, just as you would use commas. Dashes are particularly helpful to set off interruptions that contain commas or to tack on afterthoughts.

> Ex: This is precisely the kind of issue—controversial, consequential, confounding—that scholars love and judges dread.

G. APOSTROPHES

Use apostrophes to form possessives and contractions—but not plurals. Remember that singular possessives are ordinarily formed by the addition of "'s" to the noun and plural possessives by an apostrophe alone.

> Ex: don't (contraction)
> appellant's contentions (singular possessive)
> appellants' contentions (plural possessive)
>
> Not: appellants' contended (plural)

When a name or other singular noun ends in "s," most authorities say you should form the possessive by adding "'s." Some writers, however, use an apostrophe alone.

> Ex: Professor Williams's article
> Professor Williams' article

Be sure to remember that the pronoun "it" is an exception to the general rule that singular possessives are formed with "'s." Do not confuse "its" and "it's."

> Ex: It's a difficult course. (contraction of "it is.")
> The course has its difficult moments. (possessive.)

You should also note that contractions are a feature of informal prose and are therefore not often used in scholarly writing.

H. QUOTATION MARKS

Put closing quotation marks outside of commas and periods, even when this does not reflect the punctuation of the quoted material.

> <u>Ex</u>:   In addition to serving as "laboratories for national law," state courts serve as "primary guardians of the liberty of the people."

However, closing quotation marks always precede colons and semicolons.

Quotation marks should not be used around "block quotes"—quotations of 50 words or more, indented and single-spaced.

I. ELLIPSES

Indicate omissions in quoted material with dots ("ellipses"). Use three dots to indicate the omission of a word or words in the middle of a sentence and four dots to indicate that the end of a sentence has been omitted. Do not use ellipses to indicate that the beginning of a sentence has been omitted, however; the use of a lower-case letter or its replacement by a capital letter in brackets is sufficient to indicate the omission.

> <u>Ex</u>:   In conclusion, the court of appeals reiterated that its "responsibility...is not to advance the goals of law enforcement, but rather to stand as a fixed citadel of civil liberties.... [A]s Benjamin Franklin observed, 'those who give up essential liberty to purchase a little temporary safety deserve neither liberty nor safety.'"

Four dots may also be used to indicate the omission of a sentence or sentences in the middle or at the end of a paragraph. An entire omitted paragraph should be indicated by an indented line of four dots between the quoted paragraphs.

APPENDIX C

SAMPLE CASENOTE/ COMPETITION PAPER

What follows is a sample law review competition paper. Such papers often bear a strong resemblance to casenotes written for publication, differing in length, scope, and development rather than approach and format. The constraints under which a competition paper is written might compel the writer to focus on a single issue, while a casenote might likely analyze all the issues raised in the opinion. A casenote requires original research, much of which will appear in footnotes and be incorporated into a background section. In contrast, writing competitions will usually provide a student with a careful selection of relevant materials. Absent the extensive research of casenotes, competition papers tend to have fewer footnotes than casenotes and often dispense with background sections.

Generally, both competition papers and casenotes for publication follow the traditional casenote outline discussed in Chapter One, Part B(2) and Chapter Four, Part B(1). One difference is that competition papers usually use endnotes, while casenotes are footnoted. The paper that follows, however, uses footnotes instead of endnotes in order to make it easy for the reader to see how authority, attribution, and textual footnotes relate to the text. (See Chapter Six.)

Reading, Writing, and Reciting the Pledge of Allegiance:
Sherman v. Community Consol. Dist. 21

Introduction

  Fifty years ago, the Supreme Court held in *West Virginia State Board of Education v. Barnette*[1] that the State may not compel children to recite the Pledge of Allegiance. In 1979, the Illinois legislature enacted a statute which provides that the Pledge "shall be recited each school day" by public elementary school pupils.[2]

  In 1989, Richard Sherman challenged the constitutionality of that statute on three grounds, arguing 1) that its plain meaning violates *Barnette*; 2) that recitation of the Pledge in public school is further unconstitutional because the phrase "under God" offends the Establishment Clause of the First Amendment; and 3) that even if recitation is optional and the phrase "under God" is constitutional, recitation of the Pledge by teacher and willing pupils, like prayer at a school graduation, unconstitutionally coerces children who do not wish to participate.[3] The district court found for the defendant school board, and the Seventh Circuit Court of Appeals affirmed. The court held that 1) in order to "save" the Illinois statute, the court would read "shall be recited...by pupils" to mean that only teachers and "willing pupils" are required to recite the Pledge;[4] 2) "under God" is a form of "ceremonial deism" that is protected from Establishment Clause scrutiny because it has lost through rote repetition any significant religious content;[5] and 3) recitation of the Pledge is not coercive, because it is not like prayer, but merely part

---

[1] West Virginia State Bd. of Educ. v. Barnette, 319 U.S. 624, 642 (1943).

[2] ILL. REV. STAT. ch. 122, para. 27-3 (1990).

[3] *Cf.* Lee v. Weisman, 112 S.Ct. 2649 (1992) (establishment clause forbids prayer at public high school graduation ceremony).

[4] Sherman v. Comm. Consol. Dist. 21, 980 F.2d 437, 442-43 (7th Cir. 1992).

[5] *Id.* at 447 (quoting Lynch v. Donnelly, 465 U.S. 668, 716 (1984) (Brennan, J., dissenting)).

of the public school curriculum, and those children who object may select private education instead.[6]

As religion-clause jurisprudence, *Sherman* is easily within the mainstream of Supreme Court precedent. The Seventh Circuit's interpretation of the language of the Illinois Pledge statute renders it consistent with *Barnette*. Further, the court is undoubtedly correct in its conclusion that the Supreme Court would not strike "under God" from the Pledge of Allegiance. Finally, in concluding that recitation of the Pledge by willing students in the presence of unwilling students violates no constitutional right, the court recognizes correctly the simple truth that religion is different from speech for the purposes of constitutional analysis.[7] However, although *Sherman* is correctly decided, it is nonetheless, on all three issues, poorly decided.

First, the court's statutory interpretation is tortured.[8] Moreover, the court's discussion of the Establishment Clause issue is superficial: neither the majority's argument that "under God" is inoffensive because it is meaningless nor the concurrence's argument that it is only a *de minimis* violation of the Constitution seems a good enough justification for its presence in the Pledge. Finally, the court's conclusion that recitation of the Pledge is not "coercive" is reached through the unexamined assumption that the Pledge is just an ordinary part of the school curriculum. This third and most troubling aspect of *Sherman* is the subject of this Note. Not only did the Seventh Circuit beg the question by equating Pledge and curriculum, but its assumption is faulty: the recitation of a patriotic oath is in fact more like prayer than like learning to add and subtract. This Note concludes that while the analogy to religious ritual may not be so perfect as to require the conclusion that recitation of the Pledge "coerces" belief in non-reciting elementary school children, the likeness is strong enough to have warranted more thoughtful analysis by the court.

Part I of this Note sets out factual and procedural background to the issues raised in *Sherman* and details the reasoning of the majority and concurring opinions. Part II examines the court's

---

[6]   *Id*. at 444-45.

[7]   *See infra* text accompanying note 22.

[8]   *See infra* note 18.

analysis of the coercion issue in greater detail and then discusses its
failure to confront the oath/prayer analogy.

I. Sherman v. Community Consol. Dist. 21

A. Factual and Procedural Background

In 1954, the Pledge of Allegiance was amended to include the
words "under God."[9] In 1979, thirty-six years after the Supreme
Court forbade mandatory recitation of the Pledge,[10] the Illinois
legislature enacted the statute in question here, a statute which
provides that public elementary school children "shall" recite the
pledge, although it provides no penalty for refusing to pledge.[11] The
legislative history of the Illinois statute suggests that some members
of the Illinois General Assembly believed that the statute would
mandate recitation of the Pledge, and that it would thus defy
Barnette.[12]

By his father, Robert Sherman, elementary school student
Richard Sherman filed suit in federal district court in 1989 alleging
that the statute violates both the Free Exercise and Establishment
clauses of the First Amendment. School officials filed affidavits
responding that no pupils were ever compelled to recite the Pledge.
Richard's teacher said she permits no "hazing" of students who
decline to participate.[13] Richard's father stated in his affidavit,
however, that the principal asked Richard to stand with his hand over
his heart and recite the Pledge, and that other students "hassled"
Richard in the playground for refusing to say the Pledge. Since the
father did not allege that he knew these facts of his own knowledge,
the evidence was deemed inadmissible.[14]

---

[9]   *See* 36 U.S.C. § 172 (1988).

[10]   *Barnette*, 319 U.S. at 642.

[11]   Ill. Rev. Stat. ch. 122, para. 27-3 (1990).

[12]   *Sherman*, 980 F.2d at 443.

[13]   *Id.*

[14]   *Id.*

The district court granted summary judgment for the defendant school district,[15] and plaintiffs Sherman appealed to the Seventh Circuit Court of Appeals.

B. The Majority Opinion

Judge Easterbrook's opinion for the Seventh Circuit begins with a famous quote from Justice Jackson's *Barnette* opinion, followed by a somewhat confusing and incomplete statement of the issues presented:

> "[N]o official, high or petty, can prescribe what shall be orthodox in politics, nationalism, religion, or other matters of opinion or force citizens to confess by word or act their faith therein." *West Virginia State Board of Education v. Barnette*, 319 U.S. 624, 642 (1943). A state therefore may not compel any person to recite the Pledge of Allegiance to the flag. On similar grounds, *Wooley v. Maynard*, 430 U.S. 705 (1977), adds that a state may not compel any person to display its slogan. Does it follow that a pupil who objects to the content of the Pledge may prevent teachers and other pupils from reciting it in his presence? We conclude that schools may lead the Pledge of Allegiance daily, so long as pupils are free not to participate.[16]
>
> ....
>
> We held in *Palmer v. Board of Education*, 603 F.2d 1271 (7th Cir. 1979), that states may require teachers to lead the Pledge and otherwise communicate patriotic values to their students. The right of the school board to decide what the pupils are taught implies a corresponding right to require teachers to act accordingly. *See also Webster v. New Lenox School District*, 917 F.2d 1004 (7th Cir. 1990). Richard Sherman, who attends elementary school in Wheeling Township, Illinois, and his father Robert challenge the premise of *Palmer* that schools may employ a curriculum including the Pledge of

---

[15]   Sherman v. Comm. Consol. Dist. 21, 758 F.Supp. 1244 (N.D. Ill. 1991).

[16]   *Sherman*, 980 F.2d at 439.

Allegiance among its exercises.   Since 1954 the
Pledge has included the words "under God," 68 Stat.
249, which the Shermans contend violates the
establishment and free exercise clauses of the first
amendment.[17]

The court first addresses the statutory construction issue:
whether the statute is mandatory and therefore facially
unconstitutional, or discretionary and therefore constitutional. For the
court, the issue is whether "pupils" in the statute means "some
pupils," "willing pupils," or "all pupils."[18]   The court notes
preliminarily that when the Supreme Court of Illinois is called upon
to resolve a statutory ambiguity, it adopts the reading that will save
rather than destroy the state law.   The court thus resolves the
problem:

> Given *Barnette*, which long predated
> enactment of this statute, it makes far more sense to
> interpolate "by willing pupils" than "by all pupils."
> School administrators and teachers satisfy the "shall"
> requirement by leading the Pledge and ensuring that
> at least some pupils recite. Leading the Pledge is not
> optional, *see Palmer*, but participating is.   This
> makes sense of the statute without imputing a
> flagrantly unconstitutional act to the State of
> Illinois.[19]

According to the court, this understanding is consistent with
the actual non-compulsory practice in the school district.   The court
deems the legislative history "unenlightening" and inconclusive. The
anti-*Barnette* comments made by at least two state senators are in the

---

[17]   *Id*. at 439-40.

[18]   *Id*. at 442. This seems a strange way to describe the statutory construction
problem here.   Surely the real problem is whether "shall" should be given its plain
meaning or be construed as "may."   But neither "shall" nor "pupils" seems even
remotely ambiguous.

[19]   *Id*. Yet, if the court's interpretation indeed "ensur[es] that at least some
pupils recite," it is inconsistent with *Barnette*, which gives *every* student the right to
refuse to pledge.

court's view merely "juicy tidbits," politicians "bring[ing] obloquy upon themselves."[20]

The court then sets aside for last the issue of whether "under God" in the Pledge is an Establishment Clause violation, although logically that issue would seem the next to be resolved. Instead, the court assumes the Pledge to be entirely secular, and discusses the coercion issue by considering *Barnette* in light of *Lee v. Weisman*.[21] The court asks whether, given that no one may be compelled to pledge (*Barnette*), and given that an optional graduation prayer led by a member of the clergy has an unconstitutionally coercive effect on unwilling students (*Lee*), the recitation of the Pledge by willing students has a similarly coercive effect on those who object to the Pledge. The short answer is that "[t]he religion clauses of the first amendment do not establish general rules about speech or schools; they call for religion to be treated differently."[22]

The court concludes that so long as students are not formally compelled to profess belief in the content of the Pledge, they have no valid objection; recitation by the teacher and willing students is not in itself impermissibly coercive.[23] "Objection by the few does not reduce to silence the many who *want* to pledge allegiance to the flag 'and to the Republic for which it stands.'"[24]

Finally, the court reaches plaintiff's claim that "'under God' makes the Pledge a prayer, whose recitation violates the Establishment Clause."[25] While the Supreme Court has never squarely decided whether such theistic invocations violate the Establishment Clause, in recent years it has several times indicated in dicta that such mottoes are consistent with the Establishment Clause—not because their import is *de minimis*, but because they have

---

[20]   *Id*. at 443.

[21]   *Lee*, 112 S.Ct. 2649. The Seventh Circuit's reasoning on the issue is described more fully in Part II, A., *infra*.

[22]   *Sherman*, 980 F.2d at 444.

[23]   *Id*. at 445.

[24]   *Id*.

[25]   *Id*.

lost any true religious significance.[26] Thus, the *Sherman* majority concludes that like the Christmas tree, "under God" is secular, having lost its religious significance.[27]

C.   The Concurrence

Judge Manion writes separately only to take the majority to task for concluding that "under God" is constitutional because it is meaningless "ceremonial deism."

> Such an approach implies that phrases like "in God we trust" or "under God" when initially used...violated the establishment clause because they had not yet been rendered meaningless by repetitive use.[28]
>
>   ....
>
> Another problem with the concept of "ceremonial deism" is that it selects only religious phrases as losing their significance through rote repetition. Why only "under God?" Why not "indivisible," "liberty and justice for all?"[29]

According to Judge Manion, "under God" is constitutional not because it is meaningless, but because it simply does not rise to the level of an establishment of religion.[30]

II.   The Pledge of Allegiance: Curriculum or Coercion?

The Seventh Circuit is too quick to conclude that recitation of the Pledge of Allegiance by teacher and "willing" elementary school pupils does not have an unconstitutionally coercive effect on children who wish not to pledge. The court reasons that the Pledge is part of the school curriculum and therefore cannot be meaningfully analogized to voluntary school prayer, which is forbidden in public

---

26   *Id.* at 446-47.

27   *Id.* at 447.

28   *Id.* at 448.

29   *Id.*

30   *Id.*

schools because of its inherent coercive effect. In so reasoning, the Seventh Circuit correctly points out that religion is quite simply "different" for the purposes of constitutional analysis. However, the court fails to see that swearing a patriotic oath is not like studying geography—a reality the Supreme Court recognized when it forbade forced recitation of the Pledge long ago in *Barnette*.

A. Religion is Different

Once the court in *Sherman* jumps the *Barnette* hurdle by interpreting the words "[t]he Pledge of Allegiance shall be recited by pupils" to mean "shall be recited by willing pupils,"[31] the next issue is whether voluntary recitation of the Pledge violated the First Amendment by coercing recitation from unwilling pupils. This issue the court frames as whether "a pupil who objects to the content of the Pledge may prevent teachers and other pupils from reciting it in his presence."[32] The court concludes that "schools may lead the Pledge of Allegiance daily, so long as pupils are free not to participate."[33]

The court begins its analysis by asking whether "[n]otwithstanding the lack of penalties or efforts by teachers to induce pupils to recite," the First Amendment is offended by the social pressure on students to participate in the daily recitation of the Pledge and their "sense of exclusion when [their] beliefs enforce silence during a ceremony others welcome."[34] In answering this question, the court postpones consideration of plaintiff's argument that

---

[31]   *Id*. at 442.

[32]   *Id*. at 439. It seems unlikely that this is plaintiff Sherman's framing of the issue. The court's recasting of the issue foreshadows its conclusion. Ironically, the court's framing of the issue is similar to the framing of the issue in *Minersville v. Gobitis*, 310 U.S. 586 (1940) which was overruled by *Barnette*. In *Gobitis*, Justice Frankfurter transformed the plaintiff's contention (that it was unconstitutional to force a child with religious objections to pledge) so that it asked "whether...the authorities in a thousand...school districts...are barred from determining the appropriateness of various means to evolve that unifying sentiment without which there can ultimately be no liberties...." *Id*. at 597. Like Justice Frankfurter, Judge Easterbrook asks a question to which there seems to be just one right answer. *See* Robert A. Ferguson, *The Judicial Opinion as Literary Genre*, 2 YALE J.L. & HUMAN. 201, 209 (1990).

[33]   *Sherman*, 980 F.2d at 439.

[34]   *Id*. at 443.

the words "under God" transform the Pledge into a prayer and considers it simply as a secular expression of patriotism.

To analyze the issue, the court relies on two lines of cases. The first line begins with *Barnette*, which struck down a regulation requiring public elementary school students to recite the Pledge of Allegiance each day in school.[35]   The Supreme Court held in *Barnette* that under the Free Speech provision of the First Amendment, the state may no more compel the profession of belief than it may forbid it.[36]

The second line of Supreme Court cases on which the Seventh Circuit relies begins with *Engel v. Vitale*,[37] and includes most recently *Lee v. Weisman*.[38]   *Engel* held that the daily recitation of a brief, denominationally neutral prayer required in New York public schools violated the Establishment Clause of the First Amendment despite the fact that student participation was voluntary.[39]   The majority held that "[t]he Establishment Clause, unlike the Free Exercise Clause, does not depend upon any showing of direct governmental compulsion and is violated by the enactment of laws which establish an official religion whether these laws operate directly to coerce nonobserving individuals or not."[40]   The court went on to acknowledge, however, that while a finding of an Establishment Clause violation does not require coercion, in fact laws officially prescribing a particular form of religious worship, such as the New York public school prayer, are coercive: "When the power, prestige and financial support of government is placed behind a particular religious belief, the indirect coercive pressure upon religious minorities to conform to the prevailing officially approved religion is plain."[41]

---

[35]   *Barnette*, 319 U.S. at 642.

[36]   *Id*.

[37]   Engel v. Vitale, 370 U.S. 421 (1962).

[38]   *Lee*, 112 S. Ct. 2649.

[39]   *Engel*, 370 U.S. at 424.

[40]   *Id*. at 430.

[41]   *Id*. at 431.

The Supreme Court again recognized the inherent coerciveness of state-sponsored prayer in *Lee*. In that case, the Court held that a public school may not provide for a non-sectarian graduation prayer to be given by a clergyman selected by the school.[42] The court recognized "heightened concerns with protecting freedom of conscience from subtle coercive pressure in the...public schools" and concluded that "prayer exercises in public schools carry a particular risk of indirect coercion."[43] It continued, "[w]hat to most believers may seem nothing more than a reasonable request that the nonbeliever respect their religious practices, in a school context may appear to the nonbeliever or dissenter to be an attempt to employ the machinery of the state to enforce a religious orthodoxy."[44] Combining *Barnette's* Free Speech reasoning with *Lee's* Establishment Clause reasoning, Sherman's argument was that "[i]f as *Barnette* holds no state may require anyone to recite the Pledge, and if as the prayer cases hold, the recitation by a teacher or rabbi of unwelcome words *is* coercion, the Pledge of Allegiance becomes unconstitutional under all circumstances, just as no school may read from a holy scripture at the start of class."[45]

In rejecting this argument, the *Sherman* court correctly points out that "[t]he religion clauses of the first amendment do not establish general rules about speech or schools; they call for religion to be treated differently."[46] Indeed, in *Lee* the Supreme Court stressed that:

> The First Amendment protects speech and religion by quite different mechanisms. Speech is protected by insuring its full expression even when the government participates, for the very object of some of our most important speech is to persuade the government to adopt an idea as its own. [citations omitted] The method for protecting freedom of worship and freedom of conscience in religious

---

[42]   *Lee*, 112 S. Ct. at 2658-59.

[43]   *Id*. at 2658.

[44]   *Id*.

[45]   *Sherman*, 980 F.2d at 444.

[46]   *Id*.

matters is quite the reverse. In religious debate or
expression the government is not a prime participant,
for the Framers deemed religious establishment
antithetical to the freedom of all. The Free Exercise
Clause embraces a freedom of conscience and
worship that has close parallels in the speech
provisions of the First Amendment, but the
Establishment Clause is a specific prohibition on
forms of state intervention in religious affairs with no
precise counterpart in the speech provisions.[47]

Thus, the Seventh Circuit reasonably concludes that the school prayer
cases decided under the Establishment Clause do not compel the
conclusion that voluntary, school-sponsored patriotic recitations
offend the Free Speech clause.

B.   What's in a Pledge?

As argued above, *Sherman* is "correctly" decided in the sense
that it does not directly conflict with any Supreme Court holdings.
However, although the court's conclusion in *Sherman* is consistent
with Supreme Court precedent, its analysis ignores the special nature
of pledging.

Rather than examining the constitutional implications of daily
subjecting students to the ritual state-sponsored recitation of patriotic
oaths by their peers and teachers, the court assumes that the Pledge
is just an ordinary element of the school curriculum. The court
makes this assumption on the basis of a strained and questionable
definition. Deeming the Pledge "patriotic expression,"[48] the court
defines "patriotism" as "an effort by the state to promote its own
survival, and along the way to teach those virtues that *justify* its
survival."[49]

---

[47]   *Lee*, 112 S. Ct. at 2657.

[48]   *Sherman*, 980 F.2d at 444.

[49]   *Id.*

Having thus given patriotism a pedagogical component absent from its dictionary definition,[50] the court is then free to call the Pledge "curriculum." Having called the Pledge curriculum, the court can then easily conclude, citing *Lee*, that schools may legitimately expose students to ideas that they find "distasteful or immoral or absurd or all of these" as part of their education.[51] The court explains that the government "retains the right to set the curriculum in its own schools and insist that those who cannot accept the result exercise their right...[to] select private education at their own expense.... '[S]chool boards may set curricula bounded only by the Establishment Clause' even though pupils may find the books and classroom discourse offensive or immoral."[52]

By thus equating the Pledge with books and classroom discourse, the court easily dismisses the claim of coercion. Moreover, the equation permits the court to make the dire prediction that "[a]n extension of the school prayer cases could not stop with the Pledge of Allegiance. It would extend to the books, essays, tests, and discussions in every classroom."[53] The court reasonably concludes such accommodation of individual beliefs would be impossible.

However, both the court's conclusion that recitation of the Pledge is not coercive and its slippery-slope warning are based on the faulty premise that the Pledge is an ordinary part of the elementary school curriculum. In fact, a state-sponsored patriotic pledge is far more clearly analogous to state-sponsored prayer than it is to a classroom discussion or a reading assignment about a controversial subject. To pledge allegiance is to make a "solemn promise"[54] of "loyalty owed to one's country,"[55] an utterance with great emotional resonance.

---

[50] An authoritative dictionary defines patriotism as "loyal support of one's country." OXFORD AMERICAN DICTIONARY 490 (1980).

[51] *Sherman*, 980 F.2d at 444.

[52] *Id.* at 445 (quoting Mozert 827 F.2d at 1080) (concurring opinion).

[53] *Id.* at 444.

[54] OXFORD AMERICAN DICTIONARY 511 (1980).

[55] *Id.* at 17.

Indeed, the difference between pledging and learning is implicit in the *Sherman* court's opinion. For while the court points out that students may be required to "write essays about [ideas that conflict with their beliefs] and take tests -- questions for which their teachers prescribe right answers, which the students must give if they are to receive their degrees,"[56] it acknowledges, as it must, that students may not be forced to recite the Pledge.

This distinction is evident in caselaw concerned with the rights of teachers. The Seventh Circuit has held that teachers are not free to teach or not teach particular subjects according to their religious beliefs in disregard of the prescribed curriculum. In *Palmer v. Board of Ed.*,[57] that court held that the First Amendment did not support the claim of a Jehovah's Witness who refused to teach about President Lincoln and why we observe his birthday on grounds that to do so would be idolatry. In *Webster v. New Lenox Schl. Dist.*,[58] the Seventh Circuit similarly held that the school board had the right to prohibit a teacher from teaching a nonevolutionary theory of creation. In sharp contrast, however, is the Second Circuit's ruling that a teacher may not be required to lead the Pledge of Allegiance.[59]

Distinctions can certainly be made between an official prayer and a secular pledge based on the difference between the Establishment Clause and the free speech provisions of the First Amendment. Yet it is hard to reconcile the Supreme Court's recognition in *Engel* that the inherent coercion of school prayers offends the Free Exercise clause[60] (which is analogous to the free speech provision of the First Amendment) with the conclusion that recitation of the Pledge is not also coercive. Coerced patriotism would appear to violate *Barnette's* warning that "no official, high or petty, can prescribe what shall be orthodox in politics, nationalism,

---

[56]   *Sherman*, 980 F.2d at 444.

[57]   Palmer v. Bd. of Ed. of City of Chicago, 603 F.2d 1271 (7th Cir. 1979).

[58]   917 F.2d 1004 (7th Cir. 1990).

[59]   Russo v. Central Sch. Dist., 469 F.2d 623 (2d Cir. 1972).

[60]   *Engel*, 370 U.S. at 430-31.

religion, or other matters of opinion or force citizens to confess by word or act their faith therein."[61]

Conclusion .

The Seventh Circuit's analysis of the coercion issue in *Sherman* is more than disappointing. Asked whether state-sponsored recitation of a patriotic oath by school children could ever be truly voluntary, the court begs the question by replying that the Pledge of Allegiance is mere curriculum. The thinness of the court's analysis is particularly troubling because the real-life story of *Sherman* is played out in the minds of very young children. But unlike the Supreme Court in *Engel* and *Lee*, the Seventh Circuit shows no interest in whether, in fact, children who wish not to recite the Pledge feel themselves to be the subjects of "an attempt to employ the machinery of the state to enforce...orthodoxy."[62]

---

[61]   *Barnette*, 319 U.S. at 642.

[62]   *Lee*, 112 S.Ct. at 2658.

APPENDIX D

PROOFREADING

A. PROOFREADERS' MARKS

∧	Insert	=	Insert hyphen
ℓ	Delete	∨³	Insert note number
stet	Let original stand	-ⁿ-	Insert en dash
#	Add space	-ᵐ-	Insert em dash
⌒	Close up space	ⓢⓟ	Spell out (abbrev.)
tr.	Transpose	w.f	Wrong font
l.c.	Make lowercase	⅃	Move right
caps	Make capital letters	⊏	Move left
sm. caps	Make small capital letters	⅃ Center ⊏	
ital.	Set in italics	⊓	Move up
b.f.	Set in boldface	⊔	Move down
∧	Insert comma	New line	
∨	Insert apostrophe	Run-in	
⊙	Insert period		

B. PROOFREADERS' CORRECTIONS FOR CHAPTER 5, PART G

G. POLISING: PROOFREADING

"Nobody is prefect."
- The authors

Proofreading someone else's work is a demanding job that calls on highly specialized skills; proofreading your own work is that and simple misery. The only thing worse is discovering all those humiliating typographical errors after you have handed in your work. Moreover, even the friendliest reader is turned off by typographical errors and typographical inconsistencies (inconsistent spelling, capitalization, or use of hyphens.) Fairly or not, he effect of work that is carefully researched, thought out and written can be compromised if you do not allow enough time for an equally careful proofreading.

The first rule of proofreading is more in the nature of a warning: your computer's spell-check program is just a beginning. Spell-checkers are a congenial time and embarrassment saver for all writers, and a positive blessing for people who simply cannot cope with the eccentricities and infidelities of english spelling. But your spell-checker cannot detect wrong words or missing words. For instance, it will not fault you for typing "he" for "the" or "their for "there". In addition, spellcheckers do not speak the language of the law. For example, your computer will be undisturbed by "judgement" (a variant spelling aceptable in Standard American English) although in the American legal culture, "judgment" is the *only* correct spelling.

The second rule is harder to observe: read every word, do not skim. Reader anticipation is the enemy of proofreading: we see the words we expect to see. One of the most useful anti-browsing techniques simply to move a ruler or a sheet of blank paper under each line of text as you read, so that your eye can go no farther than the end of one line. Some writers force themselves to start at the end of their texts and read sentence-by-sentence toward the beginning. Whether you choose to endure this particular from of torture or not, it is a good idea to proofread the latter sections first, because they are more likely to have undetected errors. Be sure to proofread headings and epigrams as well as text. And check specifically to see that quotation marks, parentheses, and brackets all have their partners.

If you are writing for publication you *must* profread for typographical consistency as well as for accuracy; even if you are not writing for publication, you *should* read for consistancy. Foolish consistency may well be the hobgoblin of small minds, as Emerson said, but inconsistency certainly gives your paper an air of carelessness and unprofessionalism that puts off a serious reader and complicates a copy-editor's job. Be sure that all headings of equal weight are treated the same way. Be sure that your use of capitalization is consistent (If you are writing for Law Review, your capitalization must of course follow Bluebook style. And be sure that compound terms are consistently, as well as *correctly*, rendered: hyphenated, one word, or two words.

When no prefered form can be found, choose one form and stick to it. For instance, westlaw and lexis can be described as "online" or on-line" services and one of their major uses as "fulltext" or "full-text" searches. We use "online" and "full-text," largely because the latter, a newer coinage, looks strange to us as one word. But in any event, you should make a list of recuring difficult words or terms so that you can refer to it as you proofread. (You can also use your computer to search and replace inconsistent usage.)

As you may have noticed, this section on proofreading is plaqued by common typos. Go back and proofread it carefully. Then look at the corrected version in appendix d. If you missed more than one, your proofreading skills need polishing.

INDEX